Globalization, Urbanization and Development in Africa

The series offers a fresh and unique perspective on globalization and development debates and intervenes in the understudied but increasingly important field of African urbanism. Africa is one of the fastest growing arenas of urbanization in the world: it is in the cities of Africa where the interaction and confrontation with globalism, cosmopolitanism, and the future come into contact. This is an important series that is making significant contributions to the fields of African Studies, Development Studies, and Urban Studies, as well as to Geography, Sociology and Anthropology broadly. The editorial board includes key senior scholars in these fields, and builds on the high quality foundations of the former *Africa Connects* series of books. Its original contribution comes from its focus on connections: between Africa and the rest of the world, within and between different parts of the continent, between development, globalization, and urbanism, between different forms of production (economic, cultural, etc.), to name a few. The existing contributions represent path-breaking interventions into critical studies of development and globalization in African spaces and the future contributions and authors will only deepen this work.

As African cities become ever more central to the future of the continent but also towards recalibrating theories of development and globalization, this series will only become more relevant and influential. The current and future titles engage a wide geographical and topical scope that will appeal to a variety of scholars and students interested in the African continent.

More information about this series at
http://www.palgrave.com/gp/series/15438

Markus Roos Breines

Becoming Middle Class

Young People's Migration between Urban Centres in Ethiopia

palgrave
macmillan

Markus Roos Breines
Infectious Disease Epidemiology
London School of Hygiene
and Tropical Medicine
London, UK

ISSN 2752-3276 ISSN 2752-3284 (electronic)
Globalization, Urbanization and Development in Africa
ISBN 978-981-16-3536-6 ISBN 978-981-16-3537-3 (eBook)
https://doi.org/10.1007/978-981-16-3537-3

This Palgrave Macmillan imprint is published by the registered company Springer Nature Singapore Pte Ltd.
The registered company address is: 152 Beach Road, #21-01/04 Gateway East, Singapore 189721, Singapore

Acknowledgements

This research would not have been possible without the kindness and openness of people in my field sites. Their welcome allowed me to conduct fieldwork with a lot of joy, despite occasional challenges. My informants' friendships and support went far beyond their research roles. They accepted me into their lives, put up with my clumsy Amharic and always helped me to improve, were constantly concerned about my well-being and helped me achieve my research goals without expecting anything in return but friendship. The playful conversations (*chewata*) and jokes made my fieldwork a most rewarding experience. Such generosity fills me with deep humility and gratitude.

Thank you to colleagues, mentors and friends who have given me advice and friendship during this research: Ruben Andersson, Tom Chambers, Michael Collyer, Michael Gallagher, Bronwen Gillespie, Jasper Green, Elizabeth Harrison, Diana Ibañez-Tirado, Danesh Jayatilaka, Syed Faisal Mohammed, George Moody, Anneke Newman, Karis Petty, Joshua Pitt, Parvati Raghuram, Santiago Ripoll, Gunjan Sondhi, Yeyang Su, Ross Wignall, Alice Wilson, Layla Zaglul, and many others. A special thank you to Tsegay Gebrekidan Tekleselassie who has always been open to discuss Ethiopian issues and to respond to my questions about Tigrinya and Amharic.

I would also like to thank the Department of Social Anthropology at Addis Ababa University for their support for this research, and colleagues at the School of Global Studies at the University of Sussex, Haramaya University and the London School of Hygiene and Tropical Medicine.

Many thanks to Sajida for constant encouragement over the years and to the rest of our family for their support.

Contents

List of Figures

1
Introduction

The Notion of Middle Class

It was a crisp, clear dawn while most urban dwellers were still asleep. I was outside a hotel in Mekelle in the northern Tigray region waiting for the Selam Bus to depart for the journey to Addis Ababa. As the big green vehicle—with 'Selam Bus' boldly inscribed on the side—pulled up, travellers lined up and patiently waited for their luggage to be loaded into the storage compartments before boarding. Once all were seated in their designated seats and the luggage and cargo had been loaded, the bus started its journey to the capital. Soon after, the lights above the seats were switched off and most people dozed off until it became bright outside. We moved at high speed over winding mountain roads as the morning wore on, and the driver's assistant became busy responding to frantic shouts for plastic bags [festa, festa!] to the passengers who got carsick. Upon reaching more pleasant stretches of the journey, he shifted his attention to handing out bottled water and fresh bread for breakfast while an Ethiopian film played on two TV screens.

M. R. Breines, *Becoming Middle Class*, Globalization, Urbanization and Development in Africa, https://doi.org/10.1007/978-981-16-3537-3_1

The journey and its roadside breaks enabled me to chat to passengers about their reasons for travel. Two young women were travelling to attend university. A man in his fifties was going to the capital for just a few days to buy stock for his clothes shop in Adigrat, and a woman was on her way to visit her daughter in the capital. As the sun set, the bus arrived at a hotel in a small town. Experienced travellers rushed out to claim their rooms as soon as the bus driver opened the doors. Unaware that the quality of the rooms varied, I was helped by Shiferaw,[1] *a fellow traveller in his late twenties, to lay claim to a decent room. Over dinner, he shared how he had his own shoe shop in the capital and that he had travelled to Aksum [in Tigray] with his two sisters who were also living in Addis Ababa to participate in the annual Christian celebration of Saint Mary. The three had flown there together, but because of the large number of pilgrims, they had only obtained two return tickets for his sisters to fly back to Addis Ababa. Even though flights were available from Mekelle, Shiferaw took the bus all the way back to the capital because it would save him a large amount of money. As the bus made its way through the outskirts of Addis Ababa the next day, feeling tired yet invigorated, I reflected on what I had seen over the two-day bus journey: a relationship between people's movements within Ethiopia and their class positions.*

Passengers' financial position led them to travel by the Selam Bus, and their choice of this particular bus company led me to question if they could be understood as part of a growing middle class in Ethiopia. Flying was too expensive for many of the passengers, but they were willing and able to pay for the comfort offered by this bus and to avoid cheaper, less spacious and slower overland alternatives. The Selam Bus set these individuals apart from those who undertook three-day bus journeys to reach the capital, but also from the wealthy elite who paid much more to fly. On a superficial level, the use of different forms of transport appears to be for economic reasons, but the fragments of information I obtained about the passengers' lives suggested that they shared also other characteristics that set them apart from those who used cheaper buses or travelled by air.

[1] All people referred to in this book have been given pseudonyms.

Over the past decade, high GDP growth rates in several African countries have been used as evidence of the emergence of the middle classes (Melber 2016). Yet while measures of economic growth can be useful for comparing trends across Africa (Mercer and Lemanski 2020), the African Development Bank's categorisation of the 'middle class' based on daily earnings of $2–20 (Ncube et al. 2011; Ncube and Lufumpa 2015) has been widely been criticised for overlooking people's lives and experiences, as well as the role of status in hierarchical relations (Lentz 2016; Kroeker et al. 2018). In addition to reducing middle-class belonging to a matter of economics (Thurlow et al. 2015; Southall 2016; Lentz 2020, 20), such a classification is particularly problematic due to the difficulty of appraising people's exact finances and assets. During my ethnographic fieldwork in Ethiopia, it became clear that people's money was embedded in social relationsin a variety of ways and for different lengths of time. While living with my interlocuter Mehari in his parents' compound in Adigrat, I became familiar with how deeply interconnected his family's finances were. Mehari had a relatively high income in local terms, ranging from 4,000 [$216][2] to 10,000 birr [$540] a month. He paid rent to his father for his room, and together with his brother, Nebay, covered half the salary of a relative from a nearby village who cared for their compound's cattle and chickens. Mehari regularly provided money for other family members and relatives in need of cash, both in Adigrat and other parts of the country. Some of the money that changed hands was to cover immediate expenses, such as medicines and groceries, but also more substantial costs including materials for a new building and legal fees to divide a rural patch of land so Mehari and his siblings could build their own houses there in the future. Money flowed in multiple directions between people in the family as well as between relatives and friends (see also Mercer and Lemanski 2020). This circulation was embedded in ideas of responsibility and security, where individual income, investments and joint expenses intersected, and which made it impossible to pin down the exact amounts that individuals possessed,

[2] The conversion from Ethiopian birr is based on an exchange rate of US$1 to 0.054 birr (which was the average rate in 2012/2013 when the main part of the research was carried out). The birr has since declined significantly in value and Ethiopia has also experienced high inflation.

accessed and spent. Money is certainly a key factor in social hierarchies, but to ascertain its role in middle-class formation requires an analysis of how money is valued in each context (Resnick 2015).

There have been attempts to establish broader trends and characteristics of being middle class through a focus on shifting patterns of consumption that respond to the impacts of globalised capitalism. However, such approaches do not take into account local variations of the social, cultural and relational dimensions of middle-class formation. For example, Banerjee and Duflo suggest that having a well-paid job is the most important factor for being middle class in a study of middle classes in thirteen low-income countries (2008). Employment, they argue, enables people to develop distinct patterns of consumption of food, entertainment and domestic infrastructure, which enhances their human capital through investments in health and education (ibid.). This understanding builds on conceptualisations of human capital where individuals' agency and education have been considered as central to improving financial situations and enhancing social positions (see e.g. Becker 1964; Mincer and Polachek 1974). While these patterns can give a sense of some of the characteristics associated with local social hierarchies and being middle class in some countries, the emphasis on human capital suggests that social mobility is primarily dependent on increased income and wealth. These perspectives have been criticised for overlooking the cultural boundariesof social mobility by, among others, Bourdieu (1984) who demonstrated that class is often reproduced even if individuals obtain education and well-paid employment.

It is increasingly evident that the middle classes cannot be approached as pre-existing groups with clear boundaries (Spronk 2018), yet some scholars continue to refer to 'the middle class' as a backdrop and without further reflection or examination of the meaning of the term (Neubert and Stoll 2014). Ideas of a 'middle class' can be found in anthropological studies of modernity in Togo (Piot 2010) and international migration from Nigeria and Eritrea (Treiber 2013), but such usage of the term lacks analytical substance as it can cover everyone between the poor and the elite (Melber 2016). Rather than reflecting people's lived 'realities,' representations of homogenous urbanised middle classes across Africa reproduce inherent assumptions about their economic, political and consumer behaviours (Mercer 2014). More critical approaches to the study of middle classes have been pursued in South Asia (Jeffrey 2008; Liechty 2003; Brosius 2012), Latin America (Parker and Walker 2013), but also in studies of global trends of middle-class formation (Heiman et al. 2012; Kotkin 2020).

Although there is continued ambiguity towards middle-classness in Africa, scholars have over the past decade been showing more interest in the processes through which middle classes are formed. In Spronk's (2012) study of sexual relations and leisure among Kenyan professionals, she demonstrates how being middle class is not only related to employment and income, but has emerged through postcolonial social change and the local meanings and expressions of sexuality, gender and culture. In Tanzania, middle-class formation has been analysed in relation to processes of building and decorating houses that are interconnected to lifestyles, values and consumption habits (Mercer 2014). These and other studies from across the continent demonstrate the importance of exploring cultural processes rather than income to analyse what it means to be middle class (Sumich 2018; Sumich and Nielsen 2020; Nielsen and Jenkins 2020; Page and Sunjo 2018).

In this book, I move beyond neat categories based on individuals' material wealth, and question the when, where, how and why of being middle class (Donner and De Neve 2012). Instead of attempting to make claims about *the* Ethiopian middle class or to generalise about African middle classes (Mercer and Lemanski 2020), I explore how local discourses (Lopez 2012) and social, material, political and cultural dimensions intersect and form *a* middle class through the lens of urban-to-urban migration. Such migration obviously requires money, yet the crucial link between migration and classis not straightforwardly a material one. Engaging with Bourdieu's class theory (1984,1986), I emphasise how practices, knowledge and social relations transform through migration and contribute to generate distinctions between people. By doing so, the book offers new insights into 'classification-in-the-making' (Spronk 2020, 471) in terms of middle-class formation in Ethiopia and shifts attention away from narratives of abjection and decline in Ethiopia (see also Mains 2019), to provide a new perspective on the relationship between class and migration.

Class Dimensions of Migration

There is a long-standing ambiguity about the use of class in studies of migration in Africa. This can partly be understood in relation to historical claims that class was formerly non-existent in Africa, based on ideas that income disparities in the past did not materialise into social inequalities and class consciousness because of strong networks between rich and poor (Hydén 1983). Colonialism produced radical social, economic and political changes, implemented racial segregation, and also intensified labour migration (Kuper 1965; Meillassoux 1970; Clyde Mitchell and Epstein 1959), but up until the late 1950s, migration was often framed as a 'problem' and concerns over 'detribalisation' were raised both by colonial powers and the scholars associated with them (Richards 1939; Schapera 1947). This can be seen as part of a sedentarist bias in which migration was seen as a form of deviance that potentially threatened social order (Malkki 1992, 1995), and anthropologists generally preferred studying 'spatially bounded' communities and unravelling their social and cultural order, rather than the processes of change that migration often represents (Vertovec 2007).

However, the increasing movements of people made it impossible to ignore migration. Modernisation studies in Africa, especially in the 1950s and 1960s, were urban-centric and based on dualist assumptions about city and countryside, developed and underdeveloped, modern and traditional (Kearney 1986). The growth of modernisation theory led to an increase in studies of rural-to-urban migration, which was commonly explained through rural poverty (e.g. Gugler and Flanagan 1978). Migration from 'underdeveloped' rural areas to 'developed' cities (or countries) came to be understood as a natural part of modernisation and Gluckman

(1961) considered it to play a central role in what he (mistakenly) envisioned as the 'African Industrial Revolution.' Within this perspective, migrants were perceived as progressive agents of change who would generate development by bringing back innovations and new knowledge to their more traditional communities (Kearney 1986). Anthropologists working in and around the Copperbelt in Zambia and associated with the Manchester School, such as Gluckman (1963, 1965), Epstein (1958, 1967) and Mitchell (1969), provided insights into the role of migration through their attention to the social change associated with movements from subsistence agriculture to waged labour in urban industrial centres. These and other scholars contributed to a reconsideration of cultures as 'bounded, territorialised, relatively unchanging, and homogenous units' (Brettell 2000, 97).

The increasing attention to how rural-to-urban migration impacted social relations made the study of class more widespread from the 1950s (e.g. Cohen 1969; Epstein 1958; Mitchell 1969). These and other studies often highlighted how social hierarchies in urban settings were significantly different from those in rural areas of origin (Henderson 1966), and Mitchell and Epstein predicted that class structures resembling the 'Western model' would emerge among urban African populations as a result of differences related to wealth, skills, education and standards of living (1959, 36). These differences were described as the outcomes of changes to power distribution, institutions and social values (Kuper 1965), and several studies found that many people were exploited for their labour by the ruling classes in cities and, combined with major political changes, this led to a rise in class consciousness (Jeffries 1975; Sklar 1963; Wallerstein 1967). The recognition of the differentiations between people in urban centres led to a new anthropological political economy where left-oriented anthropologists turned their attention to modes of production models of a Marxian tradition (Kalb 2015). For example, Meillassoux (1972) called for more anthropological research on who controls labour and its products to analyse the reproduction of the economic system.

Over time, however, there has been a shift away from internal migration and classrelations in urban centres to international migration and transnational relations. Alongside this growing interest, ideas of Africa as a 'continent on the move' (Flahaux and De Haas 2016, 1) have emerged. Indeed, nowhere is the narrative of problem-induced migration more prevalent than in Africa—a continent commonly thought of as ravaged by poverty, war, disease and other disasters (Comaroff 2007). Migration in and from Africa is often considered in relation to conditions of economic hardship, environmental degradation, conflict and war in places of origin, dangerous journeys, and the difficulties of 'being illegal.' Research on people in unfortunate situations often brings forward critical perspectives on governments, environmental conditions and global economic inequalities, but also risk naturalising the idea of migration as inherently related to problems. The tendency to give priority to the experiences of people from lower-class backgrounds and those who migrate out of hardship has contributed to give the idea of migration a 'class bias' (Olwig 2007, 28). Migration is primarily associated with people who are deprived and seek to improve their circumstances (Bryceson and Vuorela 2002), which has shaped the kinds of knowledge that exists about people's movements. Anthropologists have done little to alleviate these perceptions as there has for long been a tendency to study 'down' instead of horizontally or upwards (Nyamnjoh 2012).

The tendency to attend to problem-induced migration has also impacted how migration within Africa has been addressed. An example of this is Adepoju's (1995) overview of migration in the continent where he acknowledged that urban-to-urban migration is widespread, but chose to pay more attention to other patterns, thereby contributing to reproduce representations of migration in Africa as related to individuals' low income and the displacement of small-scale farmers. The emphasis on such forms of migration was problematised by Ferguson who argued that the relationship between rural-to-urban migration and a 'Western-style industrial modernity' (1999, 5) in the Copperbelt was a myth that had circulated for decades and well up into the 1980s. Migration patterns in Africa are not linear or permanent, he argued, and people move in various directions for different lengths of time depending on their livelihoods and how they consider their prospects in different locations (Ferguson 1999).

More recently, there has been greater recognition of the diversity of migration patterns within and between African countries. In contrast to common media representations, only about 14 per cent of international migrants in Africa are refugees or in refugee-like situations, which means that the vast majority of migration is not caused by conflict, poverty or other deprivations (Flahaux and De Haas 2016). Instead, migration in Africa is predominantly related to work, study and family (Bakewell and Jónsson 2011; Schoumaker et al. 2013; Bakewell and Bonfiglio 2013), while internal migration towards urban centres for higher education is widespread (Adepoju 2006). The acknowledgement of the existence of a wide range of migration patterns has brought insights into how people's movements can be differentiated, such as in Kenya where urban-to-urban migration was associated with people who were employed and had higher incomes than people who engaged in other forms of migration (Brockerhoff and Biddlecom 1998).

Migration, like other forms of human mobility, is a resource and the unequal distribution of access to it produces yet more inequalities (Cresswell 2010). As a result, people's capacity to migrate often depends on their class position, and it also shapes their routes, destinations and their opportunities to prosper in destinations (e.g. Van Hear 2014; Nieswand 2011). By focusing on a form of migration that is *not* associated with poverty, but rather with higher education, employment and leisure, this book reconsiders old issues in the anthropology of migration into African cities and provides new perspectives on long-standing questions on the relationship between migration and class.

Social Change in Ethiopia

In Ethiopia, major changes since the 1990s—such as the shift from a centrally planned to a market-oriented economy, along with other factors like an absence of war, decreased banditry and new forms of transportation—enabled more free movement and generated an increase in migration within the country (Kiros and White 2004). The massive investment in expanding the road system has also played a role in facilitating internal migration. In 2012, the total length of road in Ethiopia was 63,083 kilometres, a threefold increase from 1992 when it was 18,081 kilometres, and asphalt roads increased at a similar rate over the same period, from 3,542 to 9,875 kilometres (ERA 2012). Another important change following years of restrictions and forced displacement during the period of the civil war (1974–1991) was the implementation of the constitutional right to free movement in 1995: 'Any Ethiopian or foreign national lawfully in Ethiopia has, within the national territory , the right to liberty of movement and freedom to choose his residence, as well as the freedom to leave the country at any time he wishes to' (Constitution 1995: Article 32, paragraph 1). Still, there are social constraints especially for women to move independently, while political control persists over people who intend to migrate as they are required to obtain an official letter from the *qebele* (local government) and to carry identity cards (Blunch and Laderchi 2015).

The changes in recent decades have nevertheless contributed to the facilitation of migration, and urban-to-urban migration has become commonplace in contemporary Ethiopia (Schewel and Bahir 2019; Schewel and Fransen 2018). Out of a population of 2,739,551 in Addis Ababa at the latest census in 2007, some 587,661 (21.5%) were classified as migrants from other urban areas (CSA 2007a, 128). In the Tigray region, about 6.6% of the urban population had previously lived in another urban centre (CSA 2007b, 252). Cities and towns have become increasingly attractive destinations over the past decades because of the new opportunities following government and non-governmental agencies opening branch offices throughout the country (Mberu 2006). However, this kind of migration is not a new trend and was already an established pattern of movement towards the end of Haile Selassie's rule in 1974. In Bjeren's (1985) research conducted in the early 1970s on migration to the city of Shashamene in southern Ethiopia, she identified a large number of migrants who had in common that they had previously lived in at least one other urban centre. The majority had arrived from Addis Ababa and nearby towns, and this migration between urban centres reinforced the tendency that people holding government positions and running private companies were of Amhara ethnic background, whereas migrants from other ethnic backgrounds did manual labour and worked in the service sector (Bjeren 1985). In other words, migration within Ethiopia was embedded in broader power relations and played a part in the reproduction of social hierarchies, illustrating not only that urban-to-urban migration has a long history but also that it intersects class relations.

Despite the prevalence and socio-political importance of migration between urban centres, greater attention has been paid to rural-to-urban migration in Ethiopia. Studies have demonstrated why young women who migrate from rural areas to cities face limited employment opportunities and engage in sex work to transit and achieve status of adulthood (van Blerk 2008), how children and youth migrate from rural settings to cities and become street children (e.g. Erulkar et al. 2006); there have also been studies of displacement related to food insecurity (Abbute 2004; Keller 1992; White et al. 2000) as well as war and conflict (Lamessa et al. 2004; Riggan 2011). Some studies have pointed out that men who migrate from villages to urban centres experience economic improvement (de Brauw et al. 2018), but it is not uncommon for migration to be portrayed as a problem to be solved through aid and development (Schewel and Fransen 2018; Clemens and Postel 2018). These studies stress central challenges of life for many Ethiopians, but also obscure the social realities of people who migrate for education, employment or business, and thereby how migration choices and outcomes are embedded in social and economic inequalities.

Class relations in Ethiopia have emerged out of a historical shortage of land, which has contributed to a sharp distinction between landowners and peasants especially in the highland regions. The regular surplus of agricultural production has historically supported a class division of 'peasant, warrior-ruler and priest' (Markakis and Ayele 1986, 21). From the 1890s, the Amhara empire expanded into the southern and western lowlands partly in response to an increasing need for land to sustain this hierarchy (Donham and James 1986). In the lowlands, this expansion and formation of modern Ethiopia led to the subjugation of local peoples, including Oromos, and generated new ethnic-based hierarchies (Jalata 2009). These hierarchies were temporarily interrupted by Italian rule (1936–1941), but local power dynamics were relatively less influenced by this short occupation compared to the major social reconfigurations imposed by European colonial rule on the rest of the continent. After the Italian occupation ended, the lack of major political changes compared to colonised and newly independent countries made Ethiopia a 'special' case in Africa. Haile Selassie's regime and the Amhara elite were often analysed in line with hegemonic nationalist narratives of the monarchy's rule for thousands of years in Ethiopia (Sorenson 1992), and ethnographic writing was for many decades dominated by outdated approaches and did not sufficiently represent the realities of people's lives (James 1990).

The middle classes did not fit into these narratives. Levine (1966) suggested that engaging with the concept of 'middle class' ran the risk of importing pre-fabricated concepts from abroad that were not suitable to the realities of people's lives in Ethiopia. Instead of 'middle class,' he used the term 'new elites' to refer to people who experienced more wealth and power in their lives through the recently introduced European-style educational system and who became high-ranking government officials, as well as those who had become rich from import–export trade and real estate (Levine 1966). The growth of urban centres made education more attractive as it became a path to powerful formal positions such as tax collectors, judges, police chiefs and local governors (Hoben 1970). However, the portrayal of a class hierarchy consisting only of elites and the poor did not reflect the shifts in class relations through urbanisation, new professions and changing political structures from the early twentieth century and during Haile Selassie's rule.

When the monarchy of Haile Selassie was replaced by a Marxist-Leninist military government known as the Derg in 1974, a range of policies were implemented to provide more equal distribution of resources. Whereas Haile Selassie had favoured landowners over farmers and tenants (Zewde 2001), the Derg nationalised all land in Ethiopia. This policy was portrayed by the government as an 'anti-feudal class struggle' (Abbink 2009, 9), with the popular slogan 'land to the tiller' (Chege 1979, 366). The previous land ownership system had been central in sustaining a highly unequal distribution of resources and the new system was a major shift that, along with other changes, had profound implications for class relations (Donham 1999). The policies under the Derg also shaped migration in the 1970s, wherein large numbers of university students were sent to rural areas to educate farmers (Zewde 2001) and in the 1980s the regime relocated about 10 million people through forced resettlement and villagisation programmes (Abbute 2004; Pankhurst and Piguet 2009; Yntiso 2004). At the same time, the regime restricted internal movement by requiring permits for travel between cities (Young 1997) in order to dissolve potential opposition among students and move people away from areas where they could join groups fighting against the government (Pankhurst and Piguet 2009). Notwithstanding its ambition for a more egalitarian distribution of resources, the Derg produced a highly hierarchical power structure with a small elite controlling the country's resources and population.

More recently, class relations in Ethiopia have been influenced by other ideological and political shifts. The Ethiopian People's Revolutionary Democratic Front (EPRDF), which was formed as a coalition following the rule of the Derg, held on to power through a bricolage of Leninism, Marxism, Maoism and liberalism (Bach 2011). Development was used as a concept that bridged the contradictions in these ideologies, and the EPRDF government claimed to be turning Ethiopia into a full-fledged democracy and a 'middle-income country' where inequality would consequently be reduced (see e.g. Orlowska 2013). The regime's decision to maintain the Derg's nationalised land ownership was in contrast to its claimed liberalist ideology (Abbink 2009), but formed part of a narrative of government control over resources for the benefit of the population. However, poverty and inequalities persisted despite annual economic growth rates of around 10% over the years from 2000 to 2013 (Clapham 2018). In late 2019, political instability and shifting power relations within the EPRDF coalition led to the establishment of its successor, the Prosperity Party (Østebø and Tronvoll 2020; Amare Kenaw 2020). The name of the new party suggests that it aims for economic growth and a better future for Ethiopians, but in early 2021 there are economic challenges as well as several armed conflicts in different parts of the country.

There has been growing scholarly interest in the middle classes in Ethiopia, as in other parts of Africa (Mercer 2014), though class remains a contested concept. In his study of unemployed youth in Jimma, Mains (2012) found that they considered public sector employment the most feasible trajectory to achieve the power and economic stability associated with the middle classes, but such jobs were becoming increasingly scarce and many struggled to improve their lifestyles. Others have pointed to the 'lack of a countervailing middle class in Ethiopia' as a reason for setbacks in democratisation processes (Abbink 2006, 176). Whereas such references to the middle classes suggest that there are groups that could be described as such, even if they are not as large as in other countries, Nallet (2015) takes a different approach: as there is no equivalent to the term 'middle class' in everyday use in Ethiopia, or in the country's local histories and government documents, she finds it problematic to classify people as being middle class.

This scepticism towards the use of class resonates with several scholars working across the world (Donner 2017). Some decades ago, Pakulski and Waters (1995) found that the purpose of class theory and analysis had come to an end and announced the 'death of class' because there were other models that could better explain social realities. More recently, some have seen discourse around the global middle classes being used as a political tool by global and local elites to neutralise popular protest (Kalb 2014), whereas others find that class concepts do not sufficiently capture social inequality and differentiation in Africa (Neubert 2019). Cohesive classes with clear boundaries cannot be identified as an empirical reality in Ethiopia or any other context, but this does not mean that class is unimportant (Devine and Savage 2005). Rather, class can be a useful concept for identifying and understanding privilege, inequality and social differences (Ortner 1998).

Class as an Analytical Tool

The social differences I observed during my fieldwork in Ethiopia gave me a sense that there was an 'unconscious unity of class' (Bourdieu 1984, 77). People did not refer to an exact local equivalent of the term 'middle class,' but social hierarchies exist in any human environment whether or not people think about or refer to class. Bourdieu's (1984,1986) theory of class brings together the social, cultural and relational dimensions of social life to demonstrate how each of them serves to reproduce the social structure through a diverse set of practices, knowledges and relations. Because social hierarchies are embodied they are rarely captured in all their complexity in everyday language, which contribute to the obstacles individuals face in permeating cultural boundaries and experience social mobility.

Bourdieu's approach built on a Marxist class perspective as well as Weber's insights into the cultural dimensions of class relations. For Marx, a class hierarchy relates to unequal access to resources, and the central criterion for individuals' class positions is their relation to modes of production in the capitalist system (1978[1867]). Marx found there to be two fundamental classes in opposition to each other at that particular stage of history: the suppressed workers and the owners of the means of production. At the point in time when the working class developed a class consciousness, he suggested that people would contest material inequalities and challenge the class divisions, which would eventually give rise to a more egalitarian system at the next historical stage of socialism. Bourdieu also drew on Weber's work to bring attention to culture and status in class relations. According to Weber, people's occupational status and lifestyles impacted their chances in life, including opportunities for obtaining goods and finding satisfaction (1978, 302). The simplifications in the scholarship of Marx and Weber have become increasingly apparent over time (Carrier 2015), but Liechty (2003) proposes that anthropological studies of middle classes need to take into account Marx's work to identify the unequal distributions of power and resources as well as Weber's perspectives on the role of culture in class relations. The advantage of Bourdieu's (1984) work on class, then, is that it unites these foundational insights.

Bourdieu (1984) developed an approach to study how hierarchical relations are produced and reproduced through the intersections of cultural, economic, social and symbolic capital. While Bourdieu did not provide formal definitions of capital (Prieur and Savage 2013), cultural capital can be understood as embodied in individuals' and groups' behaviour through their skills in navigating and using institutionalised power structures to dominate and exclude. Cultural capital is not evenly distributed between groups or individuals but reflects a wide range of cultural assets that emerge and are mobilised in different social situations (Bennett et al. 2009). Economic capital comprises the resources people possess and have access to through institutionalised systems such as property rights and ownership, whereas social capital reflects formal and informal networks that people can draw upon for support and access to resources, and these relations reinforce class positions (see also Li et al. 2008). Symbolic capital refers to the ways in which people distinguish themselves from others through their taste in food, art and lifestyle more generally, which is dependent on having the knowledge to use and engage with objects and relations within a system of value and meaning. In this view, class position does not only depend on economic capital, but rather on temporal and culturally constructed intersections between different forms of capital. Elites' possession and use of capital help them reproduce their privilege by excluding people from lower classes and thereby constraining the latter's opportunities for upwards social mobility (Bourdieu 1984). In a later work, Bourdieu (1986) introduced the idea that capital can be 'converted,' which breaks down boundaries between capital and provides nuance to how people can use capital to negotiate their status.

These insights into capital have been applied widely to examine the reproduction and contestations of class relations across the world. Some have questioned the applicability of Bourdieu's model where cultural features do not correspond to the tastes outlined in *Distinction* (Neubert and Stoll 2018), but Bourdieu's work on capital has been fruitfully used by others to explore middle classes in India (Utsa 2014), among Mexican migrants in Australia (Vazquez Maggio 2017) and to study religious fields in Africa (Echtler and Ukah 2015). Yet others have expanded on his work to bring gender and sexuality into the analysis of class relations (Skeggs 2004). These and many other studies have shown that there are significant variations in how people value cultural, social, economic and symbolic assets in different contexts and that they differ significantly from what Bourdieu found in France in the 1970s. In this book, I explore how social hierarchies are produced through people's possession and use of capital in different locations in Ethiopia.

Processes of social differentiation transform as people continuously shape and reshape the values of cultural practices. While there have been criticisms of Bourdieu's emphasis on reproduction of class and lack of attention to individuals' agency in improving their class positions (Spronk 2018; Ortner 2003), Bourdieu was well aware that individuals' strategies for social mobility do not operate in a fixed or permanent field and that classes are 'temporalised' because hierarchical relations and opportunities for social mobility are continuously being reworked and formed (Friedman and Savage 2017). Class relations are further complicated when people move between different locations as class relations vary and capital cannot readily be transported from one place to another (Erel 2010). Thus, instead of reading *Distinction* as a guide to social differentiation (Prieur and Savage 2013), Bourdieu's (1984,1986) work on capital is suitable to frame an empirically grounded account of experiences, practices and interactions emerging from urban-to-urban migration. Through the focus on young people who engage in this form of migration and conceptualise progress differently from many other Ethiopians, this book demonstrates how social, relational and cultural processes form a loosely defined middle class in Ethiopia.

Journeys and Relations

My earlier experiences in Ethiopia provided me with insights that stimulated my interest in internal migration. In 2006, I went to study for a term at Addis Ababa University as part of my undergraduate degree in social sciences. Soon after arrival, I found out that the start date of the term had been delayed because of security issues related to the contested elections in 2005 (Abbink 2006). In the meantime, I walked around the city, taught English at a primary school, chatted to people and dealt with the bureaucratic requirements for obtaining a residence permit. After three weeks, I moved from a cheap hotel into the dormitory on campus where I shared accommodation with foreign students from several African countries and begun my studies in social anthropology, sociology and Amharic for foreigners. Though I was not aware of it at the time, the large number of students, limited materials in the libraries and pressure on lecturers were partly a result of the rapid expansion of the higher education system that was then taking place.

I also learned about the students I studied with and their different social origins. Some were from wealthy families in the capital, one was from a poor rural area in the Amhara region many hours' walk from the closest road, another was the first to attend university from a small ethnic group in the Omo valley, and yet others came from rural and urban areas across the country. Many students lived in dormitories on campus that housed from eight up to 24 students in each room, some stayed with relatives in the city and others shared tiny, rented rooms in nearby neighbourhoods. Through my interactions with other students, I gained a basic understanding of the importance many of them attributed to higher education, their aspirations, different opinions about politics and the significance of ethnicity in social relations.

Over the following years, I returned to Ethiopia several times to visit friends and study Amharic. Each time, some of my friends with whom I had studied had moved to other cities. Their movements within the country seemed to differ from poorer acquaintances who more commonly went to Saudi Arabia and other countries in the Middle East. I became curious about the relationship between people's social positions and their migration trajectories, but especially in the movements between cities. Many people I spoke to referred to the Selam Bus long-distance coach service as the best option for overland journeys. I had connections in Adigrat in northern Ethiopia from my days as an undergraduate student, and the distance to Addis Ababa made it seem an appealing journey. At the time, this journey took two hours by minibus from Adigrat to Mekelle (the regional capital of Tigray and a migration hub (Massa 2018)), followed by a two-day journey by the Selam Bus from Mekelle to Addis Ababa, including a night spent in a hotel along the route. I envisioned the journey as a compelling fieldsite, where I could immerse myself in the social relations that were shaped on the road and during stops along the way (Image 1.1).

Image 1.1 Morning break on the road to Addis Ababa

It was with this in mind that I first set out to conduct research, between August 2012 and August 2013. However, soon after my first journey, the bus company changed its schedule. Upgrades to the road between the Mekelle and Addis Ababa enabled the Selam Bus to traverse this stretch in 14 hours of intense driving. With this part of the journey now taking only a single day, people could travel from Adigrat to Mekelle on the last minibus before sunset, spend the night in Mekelle and reach Addis Ababa by the end of the second day. Similarly, travellers going the other direction could spend a night in Mekelle after arriving from Addis Ababa and proceed to Adigrat the next morning. Even though the price was much higher than other overland options, people I spoke to saw it as a great improvement and the Selam Bus became even more popular. Prior to the schedule change, it was sufficient to arrange the ticket a day or two in advance, but with the rising demand, one had to buy it a week before the date of travel. The change in travel time meant that there were fewer opportunities to socialise and conduct research during the journey and led me to instead consider experiences of urban-to-urban migration primarily among people in Addis Ababa and Adigrat (Image 1.2).

The two cities are very different urban centres. I found Adigrat attractive for this research because I had close relationships with several people living there, but also because of its proximity to the Eritrean border and reputation for being a place with a history and culture of migration to all parts of Ethiopia. Adigrat is located about 120 kilometres north of Mekelle in the Tigray region (often associated with political power and economic privilege in Ethiopia), and about 900 kilometres north of Addis Ababa. Both a city and a *woreda* (district), Adigrat is classified as urban because its population is above 50,000 (de Brauw, Mueller, and Woldehanna 2018). Addis Ababa, the national capital, is much larger, has visible social and economic inequalities and is the most multi-ethnic city in Ethiopia. It is located in the centre of the country and is a popular destination for internal migration, which made it a natural choice for finding research participants. To conduct research in these two urban centres, I travelled regularly between them—about once a month—on buses, minibuses and aeroplanes, and spent time with interlocutors during stopovers in Mekelle (Image 1.2). These movements helped me develop a rich understanding of the differences between Addis Ababa and Adigrat in terms of population, higher education access and available jobs, as well as variations in ethnic composition and housing conditions. These insights often served as starting points for discussions with people who had engaged in different kinds of migration.

The majority of my research participants were men between twenty and thirty years of age who described themselves as being of Tigrayan ethnicity. I knew several of them from my previous visits to Ethiopia, but my sample also included people from other backgrounds, women and interlocutors who were in their thirties and forties. My interlocutors had in common that most had completed higher education, were in formal employment and had relatively stable personal finances. Many spoke Tigrinya as their first language, but the Amharic skills I had developed over the years were useful: most spoke Amharic much better than I did. Amharic is the 'national language' of Ethiopia, and many had learned it in school, been exposed to Amharic through music, movies and television, and had used it in interactions during university studies and while working in other parts of the country.

Image 1.2 Waiting for a flight to Mekelle

My familiarity with Ethiopia and ability to speak Amharic decreased the social distance I experienced, but as a tall, white man I remained an unusual character to many. People found their own ways to make sense of me, which became evident to me when I attended a wedding in the countryside outside Adigrat. My roommate, Mehari, and I walked several hours through the mountains before we arrived at the venue, where we were ushered to a table and given homemade beer (*sewa*) and a local dish (*th'olo*) served at special occasions. Like the other guests, I went over to the table where a man was registering donations for the bride and groom and gave him my contribution. As is customary in Ethiopia, donors were registered by first name and with their fathers' name as the surname, and I was registered as 'Markus Mehari.' The registrar, the hosts of the wedding and many other people knew I was staying with Mehari, but not my family background. Even though we were of similar age, the registrar found a way to situate me in an existing classification system by putting me down as a 'son' of Mehari and thereby embedded me into existing social relationships.

Furthermore, my gender shaped my relationships and made it more feasible for me to engage with men than with women. I interviewed and interacted with women on a regular basis, though there were fewer opportunities to socialise with them. The predominance of male interlocutors has influence both my data collection and understanding of class relations. Gender is often conflated with women and ignoring the relational dimensions of gender risks reifying binaries of what it means to be a man or a woman (Chant and Gutmann 2002). It is therefore necessary to include men's experiences to analyse the ways in which gender inequalities are reproduced (Hodgson 2003, 213). Even though I conducted research with both men and women, I draw more on materials from my male interlocutors but to avoid portraying men's lives as a social reality that is representative of both men and women I emphasise how performances of being a man are produced through gendered relations.

There were also other social factors that influenced the relationships I established during my fieldwork. In Adigrat, my relationship with Mehari and his family provided me with numerous avenues for finding additional research participants. Staying with them gave me access to a wide range of people and provided me with an understanding of the local context and social relations within the family and how they engaged with others (Image 1.3). At the same time, being entangled in their rural and urban networks made it increasingly difficult to establish relationships on my own and limited my interaction with people from other backgrounds. Mehari sometimes suggested that I avoid interaction with certain people whom he did not trust. Regular mentions of the term *buda* (person considered to possess evil eye) and the power such people have to inflict illness or other harm upon people (Reminick 1974) meant that I had to follow these instructions to avoid putting Mehari or his family members at risk. In Addis Ababa, I was not associated with a specific family and my social ties were therefore less constrained than in Adigrat. Still, because of my interest in the formation of a middle class, I mainly interacted with people who were highly educated and employed, and I avoided engaging in social practices that many of them looked down upon (such as chewing *khat*) (Image 1.3).

Image 1.3 Living with Mehari in his family's compound, Adigrat

Regardless of my attempts to fit in, the relationships with my interlocutors changed over time, both because of how people saw me and how I saw them. Through my preoccupation with observing, taking notes and reflecting on what was being said and done, I came to see people differently. In the beginning, I was interested in their perspectives, but towards the end of my fieldwork, I found people's emphasis on ethnicity, and their often pejorative views of other people, repetitive and problematic. This sometimes led me to avoid certain topics and, in some cases, my lack of enthusiasm affected my relationships and positionality. Although these challenges led me to new understandings of myself (Crapanzano 1977), the continuous changes in my relationships made it clear that intersubjectivity is not only about developing a shared understanding; it also involves dealing with the contestations and tensions that exist within interactions (Jackson 1998).

My relationships were also affected by my research on the issue of urban-to-urban migration and middle-class formation. Many of my interlocutors were initially confused about my interest in this particular topic and asked why I did not study migration to the Middle East instead. The National Committee against Trafficking had been established in 2012, and there were television campaigns to stop Ethiopians from going abroad without documents due to the numerous deaths, abuse and trauma experienced by many. My focus on people who had completed higher education and were relatively well off did not appear to them to be a topic that could help improve the lives of Ethiopians living with hardship, which they considered to be the main purpose of social research. People who are unfamiliar with academic knowledge production often do not see research as a meaningful activity or as 'real work' (see for example Hammond 2004), and research on the middle classes may be seen as even less valuable especially in contexts where poverty prevails.

These differences, including our understanding of the value of the research, were unsurprising, but the contestations around the value of research sometimes also made me ask 'what's it all for?' (Caplan 2003, 27). My relationships made me rethink the purpose of the research, and the feedback from people made it clear to me that I needed to seek a balance between my own objectives and how people perceived me and my research. Concerns over research objectives versus the well-being of research participants have also guided my writing. I have sought to portray people accurately, but my representation may not always correspond to how my interlocutors think of themselves or the topics I explore. Despite our different perspectives, I built their trust in me by spending time with them but also by illustrating the importance of this research by pointing to the negative images of Ethiopia that continue to prevail abroad. Instead of reproducing such narratives, I explained to them that new insights into the formation of a middle class would contribute to shift attention away from long-standing narratives of poverty, famine and conflict to generate more nuanced views of life in contemporary Ethiopia.

References

Abbink, Jon. 2006. "Discomfiture of Democracy? The 2005 Election Crisis in Ethiopia and Its Aftermath." *African Affairs* 105 (419): 173–99.

———. 2009. "The Ethiopian Second Republic and the Fragile 'Social Contract.'" *Africa Spectrum* 44 (2): 3–28.

Abbute, Wolde-Selassie. 2004. "Impact of Resettlement in Beles Valley, Metekel." In *People, Space and the State: Migration, Resettlement and Displacement in Ethiopia*, edited by Alula Pankhurst and Francois Piguet, 76–91. Addis Ababa: proceedings of the workshop held by the Ethiopian Society of Sociologists, Social Workers and Anthropologists and the United Nations Emergencies Unit for Ethiopia.

Adepoju, Aderanti. 1995. "Migration in Africa: An Overview." In *The Migration Experience in Africa*, edited by Jonathan Baker and Tade Akin Aida, 87–108. Uppsala, Sweden: Nordiska Afrikainstitutet.

———. 2006. "Internal and International Migration within Africa." In *Migration in South and Southern Africa: Dynamics and Determinants*, edited by Pieter Kok, Derik Gelderblom, John O. Oucho, and Johan van Zyl, 26–46. Cape Town: HSRC Press.

Amare Kenaw, Aweke. 2020. "One Country—Two Citizenships: The Status of Settlers in Benishangul-Gumuz Regional Sates (BGRS) of Ethiopia." *African Identities*, August, 1–8. https://doi.org/10.1080/14725843.2020.1813552.

Bach, Jean-Nicolas. 2011. "Abyotawi Democracy: Neither Revolutionary nor Democratic, a Critical Review of EPRDF's Conception of Revolutionary Democracy in Post-1991 Ethiopia." *Journal of Eastern African Studies* 5 (4): 641–63.

Bakewell, Oliver, and Ayla Bonfiglio. 2013. "Moving beyond Conflict: Re-Framing Mobility in the African Great Lakes Region." *International Migration Institute, University of Oxford* 71.

Bakewell, Oliver, and Gunvor Jónsson. 2011. "Migration, Mobility and the African City." https://www.imi.ox.ac.uk/publications/wp-50-11.

Banerjee, Abhijit V., and Esther Duflo. 2008. "What Is Middle Class About the Middle Classes around the World?" *The Journal of Economic Perspectives* 22 (2): 3–28.

Becker, G.S. 1964. *Human Capital: A Theoretical and Empirical Analysis, with Special Reference to Education.* Chicago: University of Chicago Press. http://papers.ssrn.com/sol3/papers.cfm?abstract_id=1496221.

Bennett, Tony, Mike Savage, Elizabeth Silva, Alan Warde, Gayo-Cal Modesto, and David Wright. 2009. *Culture, Class, Distinction*. New York: Routledge.
Bjeren, Gunilla. 1985. *Migration to Shashemene: Ethnicity, Gender and Occupation in Urban Ethiopia*. Uppsala, Sweden: Scandinavian Institute of African Studies.
Blerk, Lorraine van. 2008. "Poverty, Migration and Sex Work: Youth Transitions in Ethiopia." *Area* 40 (2): 245–53.
Blunch, N.-H., and C. R. Laderchi. 2015. "The Winner Takes It All: Internal Migration, Education and Wages in Ethiopia." *Migration Studies* 3 (3): 417–37. https://doi.org/10.1093/migration/mnv008.
Bourdieu, Pierre. 1984. *Distinction: A Social Critique of the Judgment of Taste*. Translated by R. Nice. Cambridge, MA: Harvard University Press.
———. 1986. "The Forms of Capital." In *Handbook of Theory and Research for the Sociology of Education*, edited by John G. Richardson, 241–58. New York: Greenwood Press.
Brauw, Alan de, Valerie Mueller, and Tassew Woldehanna. 2018. "Does Internal Migration Improve Overall Well-Being in Ethiopia?†." *Journal of African Economies* 27 (3): 347–65. https://doi.org/10.1093/jae/ejx026.
Brettell, Caroline B. 2000. "Theorizing Migration in Anthropology: The Social Construction of Networks, Identities, Communities, and Globalscapes." In *Migration Theory: Talking across Disciplines*, edited by Caroline Brettell and James Frank Hollifield, 97–137. New York and London: Routledge.
Brockerhoff, Martin, and Ann E. Biddlecom. 1998. "Migration, Sexual Behavior and the Risk of HIV in Kenya." Policy Research Division Working Paper 111. http://www.jstor.org/stable/2547354.
Brosius, Christiane. 2012. *India's Middle Class: New Forms of Urban Leisure*. Consumption and Prosperity: Routledge.
Bryceson, D., and U. Vuorela. 2002. "Transnational Families in the Twentieth Century." In *The Transnational Family: New European Frontiers and Global Networks*, edited by D. Bryceson and U. Vuorela, 3–30. Oxford: Berg.
Caplan, Pat. 2003. "Introduction: Anthropology and Ethics." In *The Ethics of Anthropology: Debates and Dilemmas*, edited by Pat Caplan, 1–33. London and New York: Routledge.
Carrier, J. 2015. "The Concept of Class." In *Anthropologies of Class: Power, Practice, and Inequality*, edited by Don Kalb and J Carrier, 28–40. Cambridge: Cambridge University Press.
Chant, Sylvia, and Matthew C. Gutmann. 2002. "'Men-Streaming' Gender? Questions for Gender and Development Policy in the Twenty-First

Century." *Progress in Development Studies* 2 (4): 269–82. https://doi.org/10.1191/1464993402ps041ra.

Chege, Michael. 1979. "The Revolution Betrayed: Ethiopia, 1974–9." *The Journal of Modern African Studies* 17 (3): 359–80.

Clapham, Christopher. 2018. "The Ethiopian Developmental State." *Third World Quarterly* 39 (6): 1151–65. https://doi.org/10.1080/01436597.2017.1328982.

Clemens, Michael A., and Hannah M. Postel. 2018. "Deterring Emigration with Foreign Aid: An Overview of Evidence from Low-Income Countries." *Population and Development Review* 44 (4): 667.

Cohen, Abner. 1969. *Custom & Politics in Urban Africa: A Study of Hausa Migrants in Yoruba Towns*. Berkeley: University of California Press.

Comaroff, Jean. 2007. "Beyond Bare Life: AIDS, (Bio)Politics, and the Neoliberal Order." *Public Culture* 19 (1): 197–219.

Constitution. 1995. *Constitution of the Federal Democratic Republic of Ethiopia*. Addis Ababa: Ethiopia.

Crapanzano, Vincent. 1977. "The Life History in Anthropological Field Work." *Anthropology and Humanism Quarterly* 2 (2–3): 3–7.

Cresswell, Tim. 2010. "Towards a Politics of Mobility." *Environment and Planning D: Society and Space* 28: 17–31.

CSA. 2007a. *The 2007 Population and Housing Census of Ethiopia: Statistical Report for Addis Ababa City Administration*. Addis Ababa, Ethiopia: Central Statistics Agency.

———. 2007b. *The 2007 Population and Housing Census of Ethiopia: Statistical Report for Tigray Region*. Addis Ababa, Ethiopia: Central Statistics Agency.

Devine, Fiona, and Mike Savage. 2005. "The Cultural Turn, Sociology and Class Analysis." In *Rethinking Class: Culture, Identities and Lifestyles*, 1–23. Basingstoke: Palgrave Macmillan.

Donham, Donald L. 1999. *Marxist Modern: An Ethnographic History of the Ethiopian Revolution*. Berkeley: University of California Press.

Donham, Donald L, and Wendy James, eds. 1986. *The Southern Marches of Imperial Ethiopia: Essays in History & Social Anthropology*. Cambridge: Cambridge University Press.

Donner, Henrike. 2017. "The Anthropology of the Middle Class across the Globe by Henrike Donner Anthropology of This Century." http://aotcpress.com/articles/anthropology-middle-class-globe/.

Donner, Henrike, and Geert De Neve. 2012. "Introduction." In *Being Middle-Class in India: A Way of Life*, 1–22. Routledge.

Echtler, Magnus, and Asonzeh Ukah. 2015. *Bourdieu in Africa: Exploring the Dynamics of Religious Fields*. Brill.

Epstein, A. L. 1967. "Urbanization and Social Change in Africa." *Current Anthropology* 8 (4): 275–95.

Epstein, Arnold Leonard. 1958. *Politics in an Urban African Community*. Manchester: Manchester University Press.

ERA. 2012. *Road Sector Development Program 15 Years Assessment*. Addis Ababa: Ethiopian Roads Authority.

Erel, Umut. 2010. "Migrating Cultural Capital: Bourdieu in Migration Studies." *Sociology* 44 (4): 642–60.

Erulkar, Annabel S., Tekle-Ab Mekbib, Negussie Simie, and Tsehai Gulema. 2006. "Migration and Vulnerability among Adolescents in Slum Areas of Addis Ababa, Ethiopia." *Journal of Youth Studies* 9 (3): 361–74.

Ferguson, James. 1999. *Expectations of Modernity: Myths and Meanings of Urban Life on the Zambian Copperbelt*. Berkeley: University of California Press.

Flahaux, Marie-Laurence, and Hein De Haas. 2016. "African Migration: Trends, Patterns, Drivers." *Comparative Migration Studies* 4 (1): 1–25.

Friedman, Sam, and Mike Savage. 2017. "Time, Accumulation and Trajectory: Bourdieu and Social Mobility." In *Social Mobility for the 21st Century: Everyone a Winner?*, edited by Steph Lawler and Geoff Payne, 1st ed., 67–79. 1 Edition. | New York : Routledge. https://doi.org/10.4324/9781351996808.

Gluckman, Max. 1961. "Anthropological Problems Arising from the African Industrial Revolution." In *Social Change in Modern Africa*, edited by Aidan Southall, 67–82. London: Oxford University Press.

———. 1963. *Order and Rebellion in Tribal Africa*. London: Cohen & West Ltd.

———. 1965. *Politics, Law and Ritual in Tribal Society*. Oxford: Basil Blackwell.

Gugler, Josef, and William G. Flanagan. 1978. *Urbanization and Social Change in West Africa*. Cambridge: Cambridge University Press.

Hammond, Laura. 2004. *This Place Will Become Home: Refugee Repatriation to Ethiopia*. Ithaca, NY and London: Cornell University Press.

Heiman, R., C. Freeman, and Mark Liechty. 2012. "Introduction: Charting an Anthropology of the Middle Classes." In *The Global Middle Classes: Theorizing Through Ethnography*, edited by R. Heiman, C. Freeman, and Mark Liechty, 3–29. Santa Fe: School for Advanced Research Press.

Henderson, Richard N. 1966. "Generalized Cultures and Evolutionary Adaptability: A Comparison of Urban Efik and Ibo in Nigeria." *Ethnology* 5 (4): 365–91.

Hoben, A. 1970. "Social Stratification in Traditional Amhara Society." In *Social Stratification in Africa*, edited by A Tuden and L Plutonicov, 187–224. New York: The Free Press.

Hodgson, Dorothy L. 2003. "Being Maasai Men: Modernity and the Production of Maasai Masculinities." In *Men and Masculinities in Modern Africa*, edited by Lisa A Lindsay and Stephan Miescher, 211–29. Portsmouth, NH: Heinemann.

Hydén, Göran. 1983. *No Shortcuts to Progress: African Development Management in Perspective*. Berkeley and Los Angeles: University of California Press.

Jackson, Michael. 1998. *Minima Ethnographica: Intersubjectivity and the Anthropological Project*. Chicago and London: University of Chicago Press.

Jalata, Asafa. 2009. "Being in and out of Africa: The Impact of Duality of Ethiopianism." *Journal of Black Studies* 40 (2): 189–214.

James, Wendy. 1990. "Kings, Commoners, and the Ethnographic Imagination in Sudan and Ethiopia." In *Localizing Ethnographies: Regional Traditions of Ethnographic Writing*, edited by Richard Fardon, 96–136. Edinburgh and Washington: Scottish Academic Press and Smithsonian Institution Press.

Jeffrey, Craig. 2008. "Kicking Away the Ladder: Student Politics and the Making of an Indian Middle Class." *Environment and Planning D: Society and Space* 26 (3): 517–36. https://doi.org/10.1068/dcos4.

Jeffries, R. 1975. The Labour Aristocracy? Ghana Case Study. *Review of African Political Economy* 2 (3): 59–70.

Kalb, Don. 2014. "Class: The Urban Commons and the Empty Sign of 'the Middle Class' in the Twenty-First Century." In *A Companion to Urban Anthropology*, edited by D.M. Nonini. New York: Wiley.

———. 2015. "Introduction: Class and the New Anthropological Holism." In *Anthropologies of Class: Power, Practice and Inequality*, edited by Don Kalb and James Carrier, 1–27. Cambridge: Cambridge University Press.

Marx, Karl. 1978. *Capital: A Critique of Political Economy*. Harmondsworth, UK: Penguin Books.

Kearney, Michael. 1986. "From the Invisible Hand to Visible Feet: Anthropological Studies of Migration and Development." *Annual Review of Anthropology* 15: 331–61.

Keller, Edmond J. 1992. "Drought, War, and the Politics of Famine in Ethiopia and Eritrea." *The Journal of Modern African Studies* 30 (4): 609–24.

Kiros, Gebre-Egzbiabher, and Michael J. White. 2004. "Migration, Community Context, and Child Immunization in Ethiopia." *Social Science & Medicine* 59 (12): 2603–16.

Kotkin, Joel. 2020. *The Coming of Neo-Feudalism: A Warning to the Global Middle Class | Oxfam GB*. https://onlineshop.oxfam.org.uk/shop/books/history/the-coming-of-neo-feudalism-a-warning-to-the-global-middle-class-hd_200156555.

Kroeker, Lena, David O'Kane, and Tabea Scharrer, eds. 2018. *Middle Classes in Africa: Changing Lives and Conceptual Challenges*. Frontiers of Globalization. Cham, Switzerland: Palgrave Macmillan. https://doi.org/10.1007/978-3-319-62148-7.

Kuper, Hilda. 1965. *Urbanization and Migration in West Africa*. Berkeley: University of California Press.

Lamessa, Dinku, Alula Pankhurst, and Francois Piguet. 2004. "Socio-Cultural Dimensions of Conflict-Induced Displacement: The Case of Displaced Persons in Addis Ababa." In *People, Space and the State: Migration, Resettlement and Displacement in Ethiopia*, 371–86. Addis Ababa: proceedings of the workshop held by the Ethiopian Society of Sociologists, Social Workers and Anthropologists and the United Nations Emergencies Unit for Ethiopia.

Lentz, Carola. 2016. "African Middle Classes: Lessons from Transnational Studies and a Research Agenda." *The Rise of Africa's Middle Class: Myths, Realties and Critical Engagements*, 17–53.

———. 2020. "Doing Being Middle-Class in the Global South: Comparative Perspectives and Conceptual Challenges." *Africa* 90 (3): 439–69. https://doi.org/10.1017/S0001972020000029.

Levine, D.N. 1966. "Class Consciousness and Class Solidarity in the New Ethiopian Elites." In *The New Elites in Tropical Africa*, edited by P.C. Lloyd, 312–25. London: Oxford University Press.

Li, Yaojun, Mike Savage, and Alan Warde. 2008. "Social Mobility and Social Capital in Contemporary Britain: Social Mobility and Social Capital in Contemporary Britain." *The British Journal of Sociology* 59 (3): 391–411. https://doi.org/10.1111/j.1468-4446.2008.00200.x.

Liechty, Mark. 2003. *Suitably Modern: Making Middle-Class Culture in a New Consumer Society*. Princeton, NJ: Princeton University Press.

Lopez, A. Ricardo. 2012. "Introduction: We Shall Be All: Toward a Transnational History of the Middle Class." In *The Making of the Middle Class: Toward a Transnational History*, edited by A. Ricardo López and Barbara Weinstein, 1–25. Duke University Press.

Mains, Daniel. 2012. *Hope Is Cut: Youth, Unemployment, and the Future in Urban Ethiopia*. Philadelphia: Temple University Press.
———. 2019. *Under Construction: Technologies of Development in Urban Ethiopia*. Duke University Press.
Malkki, Liisa. 1992. "National Geographic: The Rooting of Peoples and the Territorialization of National Identity among Scholars and Refugees." *Cultural Anthropology* 7 (1): 24–44.
———. 1995. *Purity and Exile: Violence, Memory, and National Cosmology among Hutu Refugees in Tanzania*. Chicago: University of Chicago Press.
Markakis, John, and Nega Ayele. 1986. *Class and Revolution in Ethiopia*. Trenton, NJ: The Red Sea Press.
Massa, Aurora. 2018. "Borders and Boundaries as Resources for Mobility. Multiple Regimes of Mobility and Incoherent Trajectories on the Ethiopian-Eritrean Border." *Geoforum*, February, S0016718518300071. https://doi.org/10.1016/j.geoforum.2018.01.007.
Mberu, B.U. 2006. "Internal Migration and Household Living Conditions in Ethiopia." *Demographic Research* 14 (21): 509–40.
Meillassoux, Claude. 1970. "A Class Analysis of the Bureaucratic Process in Mali." *The Journal of Development Studies* 6 (2): 97–110.
———. 1972. "From Reproduction to Production." *Economy and Society* 1 (1): 93–105.
Melber, Henning, ed. 2016. *The Rise of Africa's Middle Class: Myths, Realities and Critical Engagements*. London: Zed Books.
Mercer, Claire. 2014. "Middle Class Construction: Domestic Architecture, Aesthetics and Anxieties in Tanzania." *The Journal of Modern African Studies* 52 (2): 227–50.
Mercer, Claire, and Charlotte Lemanski. 2020. "The Lived Experiences of the African Middle Classes Introduction." *Africa* 90 (3): 429–38. https://doi.org/10.1017/S0001972020000017.
Mincer, J., and S. Polachek. 1974. "Family Investments in Human Capital: Earnings of Women." *Journal of Political Economy* 82 (2, Part 2): S76–108.
Mitchell, J. Clyde, and A.L. Epstein. 1959. "Occupational Prestige and Social Status among Urban Africans in Northern Rhodesia." *Africa: Journal of the International African Institute* 29 (1): 22–40.
Mitchell, James Clyde. 1969. *Social Networks in Urban Situations: Analyses of Personal Relationships in Central African Towns*. Manchester: Manchester University Press.

Nallet, Clélie. 2015. "Classes Moyennes Éthiopiennes Étude Empirique d'une Assignation Catégorielle Incertaine." Doctoral thesis. Bourdeaux: Université de Bourdeaux.

Ncube, Mthuli, and Charles Leyeka Lufumpa, eds. 2015. *The Emerging Middle Class in Africa*, 1st ed. London: Routledge.

Ncube, Mthuli, C.L. Lufumpa, and S. Kayizzi-Mugerwa. 2011. "The Middle of the Pyramid: Dynamics of the Middle Class in Africa." In *Market Brief*. Abidjan: African Development Bank.

Neubert, Dieter. 2019. *Inequality, Socio-Cultural Differentiation and Social Structures in Africa: Beyond Class*. Springer.

Neubert, Dieter, and Florian Stoll. 2014. "One or Many Middle Class(Es) in Kenya? Towards an Analytical Frame for Distinguishing Subgroups." In *Proceedings from ECAS 2013: 5th European Conference on African Studies*. Lisbon: Centro de Estudos Internacionais do Instituto Universitário de Lisboa (ISCTE-IUL).

Neubert, , Dieter, and Florian Stoll. 2018. "The Narrative of 'the African Middle Class' and Its Conceptual Limitations." In edited by Lena Kroeker.

Nielsen, Morten, and Paul Jenkins. 2020. "Insurgent Aspirations? Weak Middle-Class Utopias in Maputo, Mozambique." *Critical African Studies*, 1–21, March. https://doi.org/10.1080/21681392.2020.1743190.

Nieswand, Boris. 2011. *Theorising Transnational Migration: The Status Paradox of Migration*. New York: Routledge.

Nyamnjoh, Francis B. 2012. "Blinded by Sight: Divining the Future of Anthropology in Africa." *Africa Spectrum* 47 (2–3): 63–92.

Olwig, Karen Fog. 2007. *Caribbean Journeys: An Ethnography of Migration and Home in Three Family Networks*. Durham, NC: Duke University Press.

Orlowska, Izabela. 2013. "Forging a Nation: The Ethiopian Millennium Celebration and the Multiethnic State." *Nations and Nationalism* 19 (2): 296–316.

Ortner, Sherry B. 1998. "Identities: The Hidden Life of Class." *Journal of Anthropological Research* 54 (1): 1–17.

———. 2003. *New Jersey Dreaming: Capital, Culture, and the Class of '58*. Duke University Press.

Østebø, Terje, and Kjetil Tronvoll. 2020. "Interpreting Contemporary Oromo Politics in Ethiopia: An Ethnographic Approach." *Journal of Eastern African Studies* 0 (0): 1–20. https://doi.org/10.1080/17531055.2020.1796255.

Page, Ben, and Emile Sunjo. 2018. "Africa's Middle Class: Building Houses and Constructing Identities in the Small Town of Buea, Cameroon." *Urban Geography* 39 (1): 75–103.

Pakulski, Jan, and Malcolm Waters. 1995. *The Death of Class*. London, New York and New Dehli: Sage.

Pankhurst, Alula, and Francois Piguet, eds. 2009. *Moving People in Ethiopia: Development, Displacement and the State*. Suffolk, UK: James Currey.

Parker, David Stuart, and Louise E. Walker. 2013. *Latin America's Middle Class: Unsettled Debates and New Histories*. Rowman & Littlefield.

Piot, Charles. 2010. *Nostalgia for the Future: West Africa after the Cold War*. Chicago: University of Chicago Press.

Prieur, Annick, and Mike Savage. 2013. "Emerging Forms of Cultural Capital." *European Societies* 15 (2): 246–67. https://doi.org/10.1080/14616696.2012.748930.

Reminick, Ronald A. 1974. "The Evil Eye Belief among the Amhara of Ethiopia." *Ethnology* 13: 279–91.

Resnick, Danielle. 2015. "The Middle Class and Democratic Consolidation in Zambia: The Middle Class and Democracy in Zambia." *Journal of International Development* 27 (5): 693–715.

Richards, Autrey. 1939. *Land, Labour and Diet in Northern Rhodesia: An Economic Study of the Bemba Tribe*. London: Oxford University Press.

Riggan, Jennifer. 2011. "In Between Nations: Ethiopian-Born Eritreans, Liminality, and War." *PoLAR: Political and Legal Anthropology Review* 34 (1): 131–54.

Schapera, Isaac. 1947. *Migrant Labour and Tribal Life: A Study of Conditions in the Beehuanaland Protectorate*. London: Oxford University Press.

Schewel, Kerilyn, and Asmamaw Legass Bahir. 2019. "Migration and Social Transformation in Ethiopia," no. 152: 45.

Schewel, Kerilyn, and Sonja Fransen. 2018. "Formal Education and Migration Aspirations in Ethiopia." *Population and Development Review* 44 (3): 555–87. https://doi.org/10.1111/padr.12159.

Schoumaker, Bruno, Marie-Laurence Flahaux, Cris Beauchemin, Valentina Mazzucato, and Pape Sakho. 2013. "Changing Patterns of African Migration: A Comparative Analysis." MAFE Working Paper 18. London: UCL.

Skeggs, Beverley. 2004. "Introducing Pierre Bourdieu's Analysis of Class, Gender and Sexuality." *The Sociological Review Monograph* 52 (2): 9–13.

Sklar, R. 1963. *Nigerian Political Parties: Power in an Emergent African Nation*. Princeton, NJ: Princeton University Press.

Sorenson, John. 1992. "History and Identity in the Horn of Africa." *Dialectical Anthropology* 17 (3): 227–52.

Southall, Roger. 2016. *The New Black Middle Class in South Africa*. Boydell & Brewer.

Spronk, Rachel. 2012. *Ambiguous Pleasures: Sexuality and Middle Class Self-Perceptions in Nairobi*. New York: Berghahn Books.

———. 2018. "Afterword. The (Idea of) African Middle Classes: Theorizing from Africa." In *Middle Classes in Africa: Changing Lives and Conceptual Challenges*, edited by Lena Kroeker, David O'Kane, and Tabea Scharrer, 311–26. Cham, Switzerland: Palgrave Macmillan.

———. 2020. "Structures, Feelings and *Savoir Faire* : Ghana's Middle Classes in the Making." *Africa* 90 (3): 470–88. https://doi.org/10.1017/S0001972020000030.

Sumich, Jason. 2018. *The Middle Class in Mozambique: The State and the Politics of Transformation in Southern Africa*, vol. 57. Cambridge University Press.

Sumich, Jason, and Morten Nielsen. 2020. "The Political Aesthetics of Middle Class Housing in (Not so) Neoliberal Mozambique." *Antipode* 52 (4): 1216–34. https://doi.org/10.1111/anti.12622.

Thurlow, James, Danielle Resnick, and Dumebi Ubogu. 2015. "Matching Concepts with Measurement: Who Belongs to Africa's Middle Class?" *Journal of International Development* 27 (5): 588–608.

Treiber, Magnus. 2013. "Lessons for Life: Two Migratory Portraits from Eritrea." In *Long Journeys. African Migrants on the Road*, edited by Alessandro Triulzi and Robert Lawrence McKenzie, 187–213. Leiden; Boston: Brill.

Utsa, Ray. 2014. "Consumption and the Making of the Middle-Class in South Asia." *History Compass* 12 (1): 11–19. https://doi.org/10.1111/hic3.12127.

Van Hear, Nicholas. 2014. "Reconsidering Migration and Class." *International Migration Review* 48 (S1): S100–121.

Vazquez Maggio, Monica Laura. 2017. *Mobility Patterns and Experiences of the Middle Classes in a Globalizing Age: The Case of Mexican Migrants in Australia*, vol. 6. The Anthropocene: Politik—Economics—Society—Science. Cham: Springer International Publishing. https://doi.org/10.1007/978-3-319-53393-3.

Vertovec, Steven. 2007. "Introduction: New Directions in the Anthropology of Migration and Multiculturalism." *Ethnic and Racial Studies* 30 (6): 961–78.

Wallerstein, I. M. 1967. Class, Tribe, and Party in West African Politics. In *Party Systems and Voter Alignments: Cross-National Perspectives*, edited by Seymour Martin Lipset and Stein Rokkan, 497–518. New York: Free Press.

Weber, Max. 1978. *Economy and Society: An Outline of Interpretive Sociology*. Berkeley and London: University of California Press.

White, Philip, Lionel Cliffe, and Phillip White. 2000. "War & Famine in Ethiopia & Eritrea." *Review of African Political Economy* 27 (84): 329–33.

Yntiso, Gebre. 2004. "The Metekel Resettlement in Ethiopia: Why Did It Fail?" In *People, Space and the State: Migration, Resettlement and Displacement in Ethiopia*, edited by Alula Pankhurst and Francois Piguet, 92–111. Addis Ababa: proceedings of the workshop held by the Ethiopian Society of Sociologists, Social Workers and Anthropologists and the United Nations Emergencies Unit for Ethiopia.

Young, John. 1997. *Peasant Revolution in Ethiopia: The Tigray People's Liberation Front, 1975–1992*. Cambridge: Cambridge University Press.

Zewde, Bahru. 2001. *A History of Modern Ethiopia, 1855–1991*, 2nd ed. Oxford: James Currey.

2

Pursuing Progress

Meanings of Progress

With limited opportunities for finding employment after completing education and the ideas that life is better elsewhere, leaving Ethiopia has for many been the most attractive alternative because 'progress can only be experienced abroad' (Mains 2012, 8). International migration was a central meaning of progress for Mains' (2012) research participants in Jimma, but it is not its only meaning in contemporary Ethiopia. As Tekle, a 35-year-old[1] aspiring politician, said:

> There has been a lot of development [*lewt*] in Addis Ababa over the years. Since I first came here in 2001, Addis Ababa has been made again. Lots of small houses have been demolished and new, big buildings have been built. Life is progressing [*lewt*] too because there is a lot of growth, and our ways of living have become modern.

[1] Interlocutors ages refer to their age at the time of the research.

M. R. Breines, *Becoming Middle Class*,
Globalization, Urbanization and Development in Africa,
https://doi.org/10.1007/978-981-16-3537-3_2

Lewt was a word that often appeared in conversations about people's livelihoods and the conditions in Ethiopia, and was widely used to refer both to progress in people's lives and to broader and national development, depending on what people were referring to in each situation.[2] The EPRDF government framed development as apolitical and of such importance as to dictate all other issues (Gebresenbet 2014). This authoritarian approach to development has been analysed both as an attempt to 'forge' the nation and to legitimise the coalition's staying in power (Orlowska 2013), but the developmental discourse (Abbink 2012) also influenced Ethiopians' understandings of development and their own prospects. My interlocutors generally considered there to have been significant development in Ethiopia over the past decades in terms of material and social improvements and felt that these processes had made the country more modern (*zemenawi*) than it had been in the past. These changes were perceived to have improved individuals' opportunities for higher education, employment and success. Many used the term *lewt* to refer to progress in people's lives, but they also used it to refer to the development of specific places.

Both terms (*zemenawi* and *lewt*) are contested and without singular or simple definitions. Progress is often employed to refer to transformations in individuals' lives, such as obtaining employment after higher education, increasing their incomes, getting married, building a house and having children. The meanings of progress are shaped in both a social and an individual sense through people's conceptualisations of their own life trajectories. Development has similarly diverse meanings. One of the more dominant of these is that it constitutes planned social change: the processes of attempting to improve national or regional conditions by enhancing infrastructure, expanding health programmes or stimulating economic growth. But, of course, development is also the result of such actions. The meanings individuals ascribe to such processes are shaped by the ways in which social change influences their sense of their own progress. By looking at the intertwined yet distinct notions of progress

[2] The Amharic word *lemat* can be translated as 'development,' but this word is primarily used by the government and in official contexts and documents, as exemplified by the term *lemat arbegna*, meaning 'development patriot' (Gebresenbet 2014).

and development, as well as their relationship with modernity, I emphasise how people's own meanings of progress are perceived to relate to broader processes of development.

In Africa, these intersections have often been considered in terms of unfulfilled expectations. In the 1950s and 1960s, miners in the Copperbelt in Zambia, as well as modernisation theorists and policymakers, thought of development as a coherent, linear process, and the expectation was that continuously improving circumstances would enable people to lead their lives with predictable progress in terms of continued employment, urban livelihoods, economic security and status (Ferguson 1999). Instead, plummeting copper prices and widespread economic decline led to increased unemployment which forced many workers to leave their urban lives and return to their rural places of origin. Apart from a few cases of successful reintegration into village life, most of the ex-miners saw their lives as '*not* "how it is supposed to be"' (Ferguson 1999, 137). This study of how people responded to unemployment, deteriorating livelihoods and loss of status when socio-economic circumstances shifted set the scene for ethnographic studies to explore the relationships and gaps between people's expectations and shifting socio-economic realities. Over the past decades, there has been much interest in deteriorating economic conditions, especially in young men's inability to fulfil expected social roles and obligations. The emphasis has often been on the contrast between people's aspirations and the limitations to progressing in neoliberal conditions (e.g. Piot 2010).

Similar trends of decline, and how people respond, have been observed in different parts of the world. With limited opportunities for obtaining economic security through public sector employment, more entrepreneurial strategies have been observed among young men in Niger and the Ivory Coast, where people have adapted and created new meanings of progress when circumstances and opportunities decline (Masquelier 2013; Newell 2012). However, some people fulfil their expectations of progress. In southern India, De Neve (2003) found that many rural-to-urban migrants were able to improve their lives even beyond what they had expected. Not everybody succeeded in improving their lives, but those who struggled were from the lowest castes, and De Neve's (2003) study makes two points that are relevant to this book: first, expectations of progress can be fulfilled through migration, and, second, people's social positions impact their capacity to fulfil their aspirations even when they go to other places.

A common approach for people to seek new opportunities is through migration. Economic transformations and failures of development have often been portrayed as incentives for people to seek material and social progress especially through international and intercontinental migration. For poor young men in Jimma, the paradoxical conditions of material development and a declining job market made international migration an attractive option (Mains 2012, 137). In many parts of the world, migration is a means for people to overcome unemployment and other socio-economic limitations, as well as a social opportunity to enact modernity at home or away. In postcolonial regions, Europe is often seen as a 'repository of wealth and transformative power' (Andersson 2014, 19) and migration to the 'West' is often a source of status (Gardner 1995). In addition, internal migration, especially from rural to urban areas, influences status (Yan 2008). Anthropologists have also noted the stigma towards those who are not able to migrate in Mali and Senegal where women expressed contempt towards non-migrating men and referred to them as 'being stuck like glue' (Jónsson 2008, 28).

The focus of this chapter is on how people's notions of progress relate to their social positions. By examining what progress means to my interlocutors and the role of migration to Addis Ababa in shaping distinctions, the chapter provides some initial insights into the formation of a middle class. First, I provide an overview of the social and economic conditions in Addis Ababa—often described by Ethiopians as the most developed city in the country.

The Capital

When Emperor Menelik II founded Addis Ababa in the late nineteenth century, it signified a shift in state-building and an intensified urbanisation of Ethiopia. Whereas former rulers were frequently on the move, along with their armies, and rarely stayed long in one place, Addis Ababa become the first permanent location from which contemporary

Ethiopia was ruled (Pankhurst 1961). In the early years, Addis Ababa was centred around churches and state institutions, but gradually expanded southwards with the introduction of railway in 1917 and an airline in the mid-1940s (Zewde 2005). Addis Ababa was different from colonial attempts to create European-style cities and, in the early 1970s, Shack described it as a vast non-industrial urban complex with a range of ethnic groups and a highly transient population, with urban dwellers reliant on weaving, tanning, woodwork and other handcrafts for their daily lives in similar ways to 'rural tribesmen' (1973). There was little industrial growth and there was yet to emerge a major city. Even so, Addis Ababa attracted many people because it was the political, economic, and religious centre of the country (Shack 1973, 260–61). Each of its twentieth-century rulers—Emperor Haile Selassie, Italian colonisers, the Derg, the EPRDF and, more recently, the Prosperity Party—has shaped and reshaped the capital in line with their own ideologies.

Today, Addis Ababa is an economically, socially and culturally diverse city. Among the more than 2.7 million inhabitants at the latest census in 2007 were people from all ethnic groups (more than 80), though the majority were classified as Amhara (1,288,895), Oromo (534,547), Gurage (447,777) and Tigrayan (169,182) (CSA 2007). Migration to the capital is high, both from rural and urban areas. Among the people in Addis Ababa, almost half, 1,302,964, were classified as migrants (CSA 2007). Among these, 715,305 came from rural areas and 587,661 came from other urban areas (ibid.). There are also many non-Ethiopians, especially Somalis, Eritreans and South Sudanese. The variety of the population is reflected by its increasing religious diversity, with the presence of Pentecostals, Jehovah's Witnesses and followers of other branches of Christianity, as well as 'traditional' Orthodox Christianity and Islam (Haustein and Østebø 2011).

The capital is the hub of higher education in Ethiopia. The opportunities are varied with Addis Ababa University, Addis Ababa Science and Technology University and the Civil Service University, as well as a growing number of private higher education institutions offering programmes in a range of subjects such as management and leadership, medicine, engineering and computer technology. The variety of higher education options has contributed to making Addis Ababa an attractive location for many young people, and students' social position and economic background influence the degrees they choose to study for. Those in better economic positions are able to pursue higher education at private colleges or through part-time university programmes, whereas many young people from rural areas who come to Addis Ababa hoping to access or fund further education may end up as construction workers or domestic workers, both exhausting and exploitative occupations which prevent many from achieving their goals (Atnafu et al. 2014).

The differences in educational opportunities are related to broader inequalities in Addis Ababa. The shopping malls, cinemas, government offices, international organisations, UN agencies, private businesses, expensive hotels, bars, and numerous cafés, as well as the large industrial area just south of the city, are material manifestations of the city's prosperity. Individual wealth in Addis Ababa can be identified by the expensive cars on the roads, smartly dressed people in public spaces and schoolchildren attending expensive international schools, such as Lycée franco-éthiopien Guébré-Mariam and Sandford International School. The wealth, infrastructure and the sheer size of the city compared to any other place in Ethiopia has made Addis Ababa 'the prototype of a modernist urban and national enterprise' (Bonsa 2013, 194). Despite this image, socio-economic inequalities are noticeable across the city. There are street vendors in ragged clothes selling socks, tissues or stickers as well as beggars asking for alms in the name of *Egzabeher* (God) and Allah. Poor housing conditions, street children and sex workers on the streets at night suggest that the economic differences in Addis Ababa pervade people's lives in numerous ways. While there is little new about these inequalities, for migrants arriving from other urban centres in Ethiopia they are wider and more visible than elsewhere (Image 2.1).

Poverty and inequalities in Addis Ababa are partly related to employment opportunities. Education is central in shaping Ethiopians' employment trajectories and people with higher education degrees often work for private companies, NGOs or government institutions. Some years back, people with diplomas earned between 1,000 [$54] and 1,500 birr [$81] a month in Addis Ababa, whereas the median wage of people with higher education degrees was about 2,500 birr [$135] (CSA 2012). For

Image 2.1 View from a rooftop bar, Addis Ababa

people in formal employment, there are better wages, more security and prospects for career development. There are also many who struggle to find jobs—in 2012, the unemployment rate was as high as 23% (Kibret 2014). People with less education often have no other option than to take low-paid or informal work, and migrants from rural areas often work as manual labourers. Many also lack the documentation from their place of origin that would allow them to obtain the identification card needed for formal employment, while manual labour often depends on the season and is informal and unstable. Domestic work is easier to find but often requires a guarantor in case of theft or misconduct—something many find impossible to arrange (Atnafu et al. 2014). In 2014, those who could find employment as domestic workers earned from 350 [$18.90] to 1,000 birr [$54] a month, whereas manual labourers faced more uncertainty in the number of working days they could obtain per month but earned higher daily wages ranging from 25 [$1.35] to 100 birr [$5.40] (Atnafu et al. 2014). On such wages, many rural-to-urban migrants barely manage to cover food and housing expenses, leave alone fulfil their hopes for improved livelihoods (Erulkar et al. 2006; van Blerk 2008).

These inequalities are also reflected in housing conditions. Many foreign NGO and embassy workers live in mansions, and wealthy Ethiopians reside in expensive apartments in the Bole area or in villas in the Entoto hills, whereas the CMC residential area on the eastern outskirts is popular among affluent professionals. New houses are being constructed for high-income clients in large numbers throughout the city and gated communities are becoming increasingly common (Admassie 2008). Upmarket housing conditions that cost from $50,000 to more than $500,000 (Di Nunzio 2019) are in stark contrast to the many wood-and-mud huts and other forms of cheap housing that poor people reside in. The government has provided land and subsidised large housing projects on the outskirts of the city to provide better housing conditions for the low-income population, but there is a continued shortage of affordable housing. Because demand remains much higher than supply, prices have increased significantly and made it challenging even for professionals in formal employment to access affordable housing (French and Hegab 2011). These conditions have made illegal housing common among poor migrants from rural areas, and about 20% of the housing in Addis Ababa comprises illegal shelters of low quality, with limited access to water and electricity (French and Hegab 2011).

The State and Development

Development has been a central concept for rulers and subjects since the early formations of the Ethiopian state. Policies to develop Ethiopia go back to the Emperors Tewodros I, Yohannes IV and Menelik II in the nineteenth century (Vaughan 2011, 621). Early in the twentieth century, ideas of development were central to how Ethiopians perceived their living conditions: intellectuals at the time called for 'Japanisation' to generate development similar to that of Japan (Zewde 2002). Haile Selassie drew upon 'Western' trajectories of industrialisation to develop Ethiopia, but also to entrench his own power by adapting to the global system of modernity (Clapham 2006, 112). He did this by shifting power away from regional elites to people with higher education in urban centres, in an attempt to create a more bureaucratic state and centralised government (Zewde 2002). However, towards the end of Haile Selassie's rule in the 1960s and 1970s, there was frustration among Ethiopians over the stagnation of development (Vaughan 2011). When it became increasingly evident that people's expectations would not be met under the monarchy, the regime was overthrown in an attempt to emulate development in other parts of the world (Clapham 2006).

The state's approach to development in Ethiopia changed after the 1974 revolution. The Derg implemented radical national reforms to challenge existing hierarchical relations, aiming especially to transform the agricultural production system (Viezzoli 1992). The land reform proclamation of 1975, aiming to abolish long-standing and unequal power relations, nationalised all land without compensation for landowners. The land reform was not primarily a response to peasants' demands, but owed its implementation to Ethiopian intellectuals who considered existing forms of ownership to be both feudal and outdated, and felt that they could be replaced by a more modern form of organisation (Donham 1999, 27–28). The meanings of modernity, like development and progress, are shaped through people's interpretations of political discourses as well as through negotiations between a range of actors in specific historical contexts, leading to continuous processes of creating and contesting meanings.

Like its predecessors, the EPRDF government employed development as a central term to legitimise its rule. Meles Zenawi was the prime minister in this government up until his death in 2012 and was the main person behind the focus on state-driven development. Through its developmental discourse (Abbink 2012), the government framed development as the most important issue for Ethiopia. The National Security Policy and Strategy (FDRE 2002, 5–6) posited development to be fundamental to the continued existence of the Ethiopian state as well as for Ethiopians to live 'free from poverty, ignorance and backwardness.' The government used words such as *tsere-dehenet tegel* (anti-poverty struggle), *lemat arbegna* (development patriot) and *jegna* (hero) in a militarised discourse to accentuate the importance of development (Gebresenbet 2014). The EPRDF government claimed to be the only actor with developmental credentials and civil society organisations, opposition groups and private enterprises were portrayed as rent-seeking (Rahmato 2011, 8–9). 'Rent-seeker' became a political insult that indicated someone who is seeking personal gain over development (Vaughan and Gebremichael 2011), and the term *tserelemat* (anti-development) was used in similar ways (Gebresenbet 2014). These terms reveal the morally loaded and highly politicised discourse about development.

The EPRDF government's developmental discourse was also directed towards the wider Ethiopian population and had significant implications on people's lives. The war against the Derg led by the Tigray People's Liberation Front (TPLF), where Meles Zenawi became a key figure, was largely a peasant revolution (Young 1997) and, after coming to power, the EPRDF initially focused its development policies to benefit the approximately 85% of the population that depended on rural agricultural production. The Agricultural Development-Led Industrialisation (ADLI) policy from 1993 guided the initial formation of the developmental state. Ethiopia was understood by its government as a 'labour-rich and capital-poor country' where non-mechanised agriculture should continue alongside the widespread introduction of irrigation, fertiliser and improved seeds (Lavers 2012, 109). This approach was expected to increase agricultural productivity and stimulate demand for domestic production of farming tools, fertiliser and consumption goods (Lavers 2012), and thereby generate a broader process of development. EPRDF policymakers' interest in rural development gradually widened to include a form of urban development based on free enterprise, foreign investment and industrial parks, especially from 2000 onwards (Lefort 2015). Consequently, the capital and other urban centres saw large population growth, upgrades to infrastructure and transportation, and an expansion of the education and health systems (Dorosh and Schmidt 2010). These policies can be seen in relation to the government's broader emphasis on development and on turning Ethiopia into a middle-income country (see Clapham (2018) and Abbink (2017) for background and in-depth analyses of the Ethiopian developmental state).

The EPRDF government justified its authoritarian development policies partly by drawing on well-known narratives of Ethiopian history. The construction of the biggest water reservoir in Africa, the Grand Ethiopian Renaissance Dam (also known as the Millennium Dam), is regularly depicted on recharging cards for mobile phones and on other everyday items, and the new dam has been equalled to historical icons such as Gondar castle and the Aksum obelisks in creating an identity for the modern Ethiopian nation (Orlowska 2013). The celebrations of the Ethiopian millennium in 2007 were used to convey how the country could be developed by building upon its history.

Through such rhetoric and symbolism, the government contested the past (Triulzi 2006) and politicised development. These processes of recreating the nation through narratives about the past and the future demonstrate how the government sought to legitimise its own role in developing Ethiopia. The government's approach and discourse around development contributed to make the idea ubiquitous and thereby influenced how people think about their own opportunities to progress. This hegemonic developmental discourse gradually becomes an internalised set of assumptions for many people (de Waal 2013). Whereas de Waal (2013) finds that people have accepted the discourse, Abbink suggests that the authoritarian implementation of development leaves little room for contestation. Ethiopians who had been affected by and objected to the construction of yet another dam in the south of the country were silenced, as the government grounded its political practices in global developmental discourse to reinvent coercive state legitimacy (Abbink 2012). State-led development in Ethiopia was non-participatory and central authorities made policy decisions and programme choices without being held accountable by anyone (Rahmato 2011, 8–9). The authoritarian approach to development was further complicated by the EPRDF's ideological stance. The justification for implementing neoliberal reforms in Ethiopia was to strengthen democracy, the economy and individual freedom, while at the same time activists were persecuted and economic inequalities grew (Ellison 2009, 89). In other words, development became an ideology that was used flexibly to suppress dissenting voices and opposition. Growing opposition to the EPRDF government and its authoritarian rule culminated in large-scale protests and a state of emergency in 2016, which eventually led to changes in the power within the party and Abiy Ahmed becoming the first prime minister representing the Oromo part of the EPRDF coalition in 2018.

The contrasts between the developmental discourse and the continued poverty, lack of employment and other challenges have influenced how people in Ethiopia conceptualise national development as well as their own progress. Ethiopians have responded differently to the developmental discourse, but for many who face poor prospects to sustain or improve their lives locally, migration is associated with progress and international migration is an appealing option for some poor rural dwellers. Internal migrants in Ethiopia tend to be better educated than those who do not migrate (Bezu and Holden 2014; Tegegne and Penker 2016) and for the interlocutors of this book urban-to-urban migration was a more attractive option than going overseas, and one which, in the following, I consider in relation to the formation of a middle class.

City People

Haftay was 26 years old and had his own photo studio in Adigrat. During his teenage years, he lived with his father in several towns in Tigray for about a year in each place, and completed his A levels in information technology in Mekelle before returning to Adigrat at the age of 18. He moved back in with his parents and younger siblings in the rural area where he had spent his childhood years, just outside the city, and soon found employment as a computer teacher for teenagers in a religious organisation. After about two years in this job, he set up a stationery store in central Adigrat with nine friends through a government-supported initiative to employ young people in cooperatives. It soon became clear that the surplus was too low for all 10 associates to make a living, and when they split the cooperative, Haftay turned the store into his own photo studio. He filmed weddings and other events, designed banners and advertisements for local businesses and took portrait photos. Haftay sometimes made as much as 10,000 birr [$540] a month and was renting an apartment in central Adigrat. He lived on his own and had a domestic worker who came by in the morning to prepare his breakfast and lunch but he went out for dinner in restaurants every evening. Even though he came from a poor rural background, Haftay had been able to establish himself as a prosperous businessman and frequented Adigrat's bars more or less every evening. To him, city life offered a variety of conditions that were superior to rural life:

> If you stay for a long time in the city and then go to the countryside, it's difficult to get along with people from the countryside. It's easy to move from the countryside to the city, but almost impossible to move the other way. In the city, you can do business, dress up in nice clothes and wear good shoes. You also get to know many people from different places and share ideas with them. In the countryside, you will eat with your family and be alone. It's difficult to get to know new people and people's perspectives are all the same.

Indeed, the countryside was generally perceived to be backward and to offer lower quality of life. In bigger cities, my interlocutors found that there were better work opportunities and material conditions, as well as wider diversity that would enable them to become more knowledgeable of the world. To Haftay, the modernity (*zemenawinet*) of city life was reflected in the opportunities to meet and learn from people from different places, buy clothes and make money.

Many shared this perspective, but also spoke about variations between different Ethiopian cities. After completing a higher education degree in the south of Ethiopia, Samuel, aged 28, had moved to Mekelle to work as a lecturer at the university. He told me why the conditions for progress differed between Mekelle and Adigrat:

> *Samuel*: In Mekelle, there are lots of opportunities for work. There are lots of educated people, there is access.
> *Markus*: Access to what?
> *Samuel*: Access to work, there are lots of people and when there are lots of people demand is created. For example, every day people use the internet and if it is fast people will use it. They make internet faster because of competition. Here in Adigrat there is little competition and the internet is very slow.

Many interlocutors used the English word 'access' even in Amharic conversations. This use of English was itself a reflection of social position and an expression of modernity (see Jayadeva 2018 for an account of how the middle classes in India use English to distinguish themselves from lower classes). To Samuel, 'access' meant opportunities for living a more fulfilling life, and that Mekelle was more developed than Adigrat. Like Samuel, Tesfay had lived in different cities and towns in Ethiopia and associated access primarily with big cities: 'There is access to everything in Addis Ababa!' This abstract concept had different meanings, but all its variations were associated with development and modernity.

Corresponding with this view of bigger cities, many considered there to be less access in small places because of the comparative lack of development. Senait was in her mid-twenties and lived in Adigrat. She had completed a bachelor's degree in journalism and communications at Bahir Dar University before returning to Adigrat. Within two months, she found employment as a communication officer for an NGO where she met and started a relationship with a colleague from Europe. After some time she moved in with him and his high income allowed her to quit her job and pursue full-time studies for a master's degree in development studies at Mekelle University. Towards the end of her studies, the two were married and she returned to write her dissertation in Adigrat. She had grown up in poor conditions with her grandmother, but through higher education, Senait had been able to obtain employment, expand her social networks and pursue a second degree. These experiences had influenced how she viewed different places:

> Adigrat is not a convenient place for progress. Adigrat is small and there is limited access. Many people have work, but they will stay in one job their whole life because they can't see any better alternatives. This makes them sleepy and they don't progress.

Like Samuel and Tesfay, Senait referred to access as a property that defined locations and influenced individuals' lifestyles and attitudes. Whereas the access available in big cities would provide people with opportunities to change their ways of living, the perception of a place like Adigrat as backwards was that it not only limited people's capacity to improve their lives, but also their aspirations.

Many also mentioned the diversity of people in large cities. Tesfay had lived in different parts of Ethiopia and found the exposure to people from diverse backgrounds enriching:

> If I live in Addis Ababa, I will meet people from Bahir Dar, from Jimma, from Harar, from USA, from Norway. I would like to live in such situation because I want to have contact with a lot of people from different backgrounds with different knowledge, different culture, different awareness, and different languages. Such conditions give you a broader awareness. In Tigray, we are very similar and if I stay here, I won't learn anything new.

Migration to bigger cities would enable my interlocutors to engage more directly with better access and diversity. Like Haftay who explained the social value of living in the city over rural areas, Tesfay considered the engagement with people from different backgrounds to be valuable in itself because it made it possible to learn and develop new perspectives on the world. His account of the importance of gaining new insights from social interactions shows that diversity was an attractive factor to him, but also that there were more opportunities for engaging with people from different cities and countries in a place like Addis Ababa than in Adigrat. These encounters with diversity were considered to impact on people and their knowledge by making them more aware of the world beyond their place of origin.

People who had little or no experience of migration noticed these transformations in migrants when they returned. Apart from one trip to Mekelle, Lemlem, a 22-year-old woman, had hardly been outside of Adigrat, whereas most of her peers had left:

> Only a few of my friends from school remain in Adigrat. Most them have gone to Mekelle or Addis Ababa. When people go to other places, their perspectives change and they become more knowledgeable. They develop their perspectives and become city people [*yeketema saw*].

Lemlem's observation of how people changed when they went elsewhere indicates that she considered migrants' engagements with access and diversity in more developed places to widen their perspectives of the world in ways that turned them into city people. On the other hand, people with little or no migration experience, like herself, remained unchanged. The individual transformations of migrants not only contributed to making them distinct from those who were more 'stationary,' but also suggests that, for my interlocutors, a closer association with larger cities meant progress.

Choosing Internal Migration

Individuals' prospects for material improvement were tied to particular spaces. Whereas migration to more developed places provided access and diversity for my interlocutors, there were also inequalities in the cities they migrated to. Elias was a 28-year-old doctor from Tembien in eastern Tigray who had worked in Adigrat before moving to Addis Ababa to train for specialisation. After living there for about a year, he was still surprised at how many people struggled to get by:

> Investors are building big buildings and the government focuses on infrastructure and making roads, but there are people who don't eat and don't drink. I thought that all people in Addis Ababa live a good life, but when

> I came here I saw all the problems and that there are many people who don't live well. There is a big gap between rich and poor, many people are left behind. It's necessary to make these people progress.

People who continued to live in poverty despite Ethiopia's development and supposedly widening opportunities for progress were sometimes termed *hwalaqer*, which means 'backward.' Material inequalities were very visible in Addis Ababa and countered many people's expectations of a more developed city. This discovery also gave them more nuanced expectations of their own potential for progress in Ethiopia but internal migration remained the preference for most of my interlocutors.

There were also people who were backward behind in a social sense, which was another meaning of the term. Petros, aged 24, who had studied at Gondar University and had returned to live in Adigrat, pointed out that migrants were different from non-migrants: 'When my friends who have gone to Addis Ababa come back for holidays, they joke and say that Adigrat is the land of mountains and country bumpkins [*yeteraraena yefara hager*].' Those who did not migrate remained backward, both in a physical and in a social sense, which was in opposition to those who migrated to attractive urban centres and became city people. These prospects were central to my interlocutors' reflections about migration to bigger cities. As Petros said:

> There is a lot of choice there [Addis Ababa], many new things to experience. It makes me happy to see new things. Here in Adigrat life is easy because it's cheap to live here, but it's boring. There won't be any new things and I don't have any expectations for progress here.

The lack of opportunities to progress in Adigrat was perceived to be a result of its limited development, whereas living in a place with access and diversity would enable my interlocutors to change their lives in ways that were inconceivable in a small town (Image 2.2).

Experiences of migration supported the perceptions of different cities' impact on people. Medhane, a 28-year-old man from Adigrat had recently migrated to Addis Ababa and found that living in the capital had already influenced him: 'It's better here because you become strong. I've

Image 2.2 Mountain surrounding Adigrat

learned a lot in seven months. In Tigray, I lived a simple life, drinking beer and sitting around, but you don't learn anything in that way.' To Medhane, the shift from his former behaviour constituted progress. By migrating to Addis Ababa and pursuing new forms of employment, as well as living in a place with access and diversity, Medhane considered himself to be in the process of becoming a different kind of person from those who did not migrate. His account captures the central reasons given by my interlocutors for migrating internally: opportunities to learn new skills and to become resilient and more knowledgeable of other urban lifestyles. The logic underlying the value people attributed to these elements is the pursuit of status through increasing symbolic capital, which highlights how distinctions are shaped through culturally constructed meanings and norms. The trend among my interlocutors of preferring internal migration contrasts to those of the young menwhom Mains (2012) worked with, for whom international migration became the most feasible means to overcome what they saw as the backwardness of Ethiopia and to reconstruct their personal relationships to development.

There is no doubt that many Ethiopians have and continue to go abroad. In the 1970s and 1980s, Ethiopia was one of the world's top producers of refugees due to civil war and drought (Levine 2004), and many ended up in neighbouring countries (Bulcha 1988; Kibreab 1996). Today, many Ethiopians migrate to the Gulf, South Africa and other parts of the world (e.g. de Regt 2010; Gebre, Maharaj, and Pillay 2010). My interlocutors' perspectives differed from narratives about international migration as the most attractive form of migration for Africans and, in fact, several considered the prospect of going abroad rather unappealing. My roommate in Adigrat, Mehari, was in his late twenties and lived in his family's compound. He had studied for a bachelor's degree in business management at Jimma University in southwestern Ethiopia but fled the city in his final year without completing the degree after becoming entangled in ethnic conflicts related to the 2005 elections. He went to Addis Ababa to stay with his elder sister, Rahel, and began working in her stationery store close to the Mercato neighbourhood. After two years of working long days with little pay, he moved back to his native Adigrat. His elder brother, Nebay, helped him find temporary employment at a government-led food security programme. After the project came to an end, he obtained employment as a guide for tourists trekking in the mountains of Tigray. However, Mehari's somewhat unusual career trajectory and lack of job security, did not mean that going abroad was an option for him:

> I don't want to go abroad. I haven't thought about doing it, I want freedom. It doesn't seem to me that I can be free like I can in my own country if I go abroad. For example, many people who go from here they don't find good work, they become taxi drivers and domestic workers. They only get bad work [*metfo sera*]. I don't want to live like that, it's better for me here.

Mehari accentuated this point by telling me that international migrants were sometimes referred jokingly to as 'ground technicians.' He elaborated by pointing out that many people lied about their jobs abroad:

'Everybody knows that they work on the ground, but as cleaners and in other bad jobs.' By referring to them with a term that reflected inferior work 'on the ground,' he contested their status as international migrants and suggested that the value of their increased economic capital was less because of how it was obtained (for a similar case related to Zimbabweans in the United Kingdom, see McGregor 2007). My interlocutors' attitudes towards employment opportunities abroad and the people who undertook international migration show that there is not necessarily a direct relationship between economic capital and status. Instead, the conversion of economic capital into symbolic capital depends on individuals' cultural capital: their ability to read each situation and to maximise the status enhancement from such processes.

Many young people in Ethiopia aspire to migrate. However, the majority consider migration to larger urban centres more attractive than going abroad (Schewel and Fransen 2018). Another research participant, Elsa, a 24-year-old woman from Adigrat living in Mekelle and working for an international company, had also chosen to stay in Ethiopia. She had seen the consequences of international migration and had no interest in pursuing it herself:

> I have seen people who come back with mental health problems. Especially those who go to Saudi Arabia are affected, but also some who have been to Europe and the US have problems with the mind. Many Ethiopians end up doing lower work [*zeqetegna sera*] and only get to rest three or four hours a night, especially in Arab countries. This hurts them and those who end up in such hard conditions worry a lot. If you go without any family and have no support, it is difficult and you can lose your sanity.

Among my interlocutors, it was common to obtain relatively well-paid and permanent employment in Ethiopia after completing higher education. To them, working conditions abroad overshadowed the prospects for accumulating wealth, not only because of the dangers but also because they would be looked down upon for going to places associated with demeaning working conditions. The jobs that were open to Ethiopians abroad, especially in the Middle East, were mainly as drivers and domestic workers, which my interlocutors considered bad, low-status work. Such international migration would not enable them to overcome the 'backwardness' of Ethiopia (Mains 2012) and would not constitute upward social mobility even if they earned more money because of the association with low-status work.

Yet many rural and poor urban Ethiopians continue to engage in international migration despite the perils of irregular migration and the difficult working conditions in other countries. People I engaged with were empathetic towards those who decided to try to make a better life for themselves abroad. Haftay, who had set up the photo studio in Adigrat, said:

> People go abroad because there is no work or because they don't make enough money from the work they do. Or if their hope is cut. Some people see no solution and think they might as well die, saying: 'either I die or I become rich'. The people who say this think it's better to die than to live like this, and it's true for those who have no work.

This perspective on international migration illustrates another dimension of how migration shapes social distinctions. Haftay's understanding of why some engaged in irregular international migration reveals that he associated this pattern with people who were unable to live worthwhile lives in Ethiopia. For them, going abroad was not a threat to their already low status, but offered an opportunity to enhance their economic capital. Such an improvement could potentially change their lives; it might mean progress to them, but not to Haftay and other people in similar positions. Progress was a ubiquitous idea among many Ethiopians, but its meaning varied depending on social position (Image 2.3).

Even though my interlocutors showed little interest in international migration, it was obvious to them that the opportunities for becoming rich were greater in Europe and North America than in Ethiopia. There was a big difference between those who migrated there and those who went to the Middle East, and the local urban environment was partly reshaped through remittances from abroad. As Senait said: 'Many people come back with money and some send money before they return. One can see how the houses of the families of those who have gone abroad

Image 2.3 Bank advertising billboard, Adigrat: 'For the realisation of your vision'

have changed and improved.' Most people were familiar with whose houses had been amended through remittances from abroad, both in Adigrat and in other places. Some migrants financed cafes and bars and named them after the European and North American cities where they had lived and Haftay said that the 'diaspora builds houses, give money to their families, to organisations and also give students scholarships.' This generosity and investment generated perceptions of great economic prospects in some parts of the world, and made it clear that there were jobs that paid higher salaries than what was available to most people in Ethiopia.

When I asked Haftay if he was jealous of the wealth people accumulated abroad, he responded: 'Of course, everybody is jealous of the diaspora.' Obviously, most people wanted to become richer, but the social costs of increasing economic capital through international migration were too high for him and others. In addition to the issue of bad work, international migrants who became richer were not unequivocally appreciated:

> My uncle went to the United States thirty years ago, during the Derg. He sometimes comes to visit and, like other people who live abroad, he is a bit difficult. People's behaviour change, they become arrogant [*kurategna*] because they have money. Everybody is poor here in comparison and they feel above us. Even those who've been to Saudi Arabia change and become arrogant.

Haftay's disapproval of international migrants' claims to superiority over those who stayed in Ethiopia illustrates that increasing wealth did not always equal status (see also Mercer and Lemanski 2020). Increasing global connections have made international migration attractive to many young people in Africa (Graw and Schielke 2012), but wealth obtained through bad, low-status work abroad did not mean progress to my interlocutors. The perceived negative changes in international migrants' personalities also put them off such ideas. People made distinctions between migrants depending on their destinations. To my interlocutors, the appeal of migrating to other cities within Ethiopia was related to how such experiences would expand their perspectives, alter their relationships with other people and enhance their status. Thus, their aspirations for destinations within Ethiopia, can be seen in relation to the distinct meanings they ascribed to progress.

Progress in Ethiopia

The developmental discourse in Ethiopia has shaped people's understandings of social change and made progress a pervasive idea. The social, economic and material transformations of Ethiopia have influenced what people consider to be meaningful lives and how they should improve over time. Anthropological research in African contexts has often argued that widespread economic decline and the privatisation of the public sector have decreased opportunities for people to achieve their expectations (e.g. Masquelier 2013; Hansen 2005; Ferguson 1999). To my interlocutors, leaving the smaller cities they considered to be backward was a means to overcome the limited prospects for progress as bigger cities were associated with access and diversity, which not only gave them new experiences but also widened their knowledge. These conceptualisations of progress, and how it could be achieved in Ethiopia, were very different from those who felt that their prospects would be better abroad. The research trend that focuses on international migration (e.g. de Regt 2010; Fernandez 2010) reflects the broader tendency of primarily researching poor people in Ethiopia, but a different narrative of progress emerges when attending to migrants who proactively choose to avoid dangerous international migration.

Although international migration could make my interlocutors richer, increasing wealth alone did not mean progress to them. Rather than making them 'city people' to be looked up to, like the internal migrants who went to bigger cities, the bad work and poor quality of life, especially in neighbouring countries and the Middle East, would actually reduce their status. Migration further afield, to Europe and the United States, could increase migrants' economic capital and carried higher status, but many referred to those who did migrate to such places as having been negatively impacted by these experiences. Clearly, the possibility to earn more money abroad was an attraction to many. Higher levels of incomecan increase people's aspirations and opportunities to migrate (De Haas 2007), but wealthier people are also often in better positions to achieve their aspirations where they are (Schewel 2015). When weighed against the social cost and loss of status, however, my interlocutors decided against this option. This was related to the social value of economic capital which depended on a hierarchy of migration destinations. For them, it was migration within the country that was the most feasible trajectory for enhancing their social positions (Lentz 2020). People who migrate abroad can experience a 'status paradox' due to the sudden shifts in their social position in new contexts (Nieswand 2011), and in Ethiopia, migrants returning from abroad with increased economic capital were not always able to translate it into the status they expected.

What progress means is a cultural construct that is embedded in class relations. The contextual values of migration further suggest that the ways in which people construed and acted upon these meanings shaped social distinctions between people. The experiences of more diverse cities and the knowledge of lifestyles associated with more developed places contributed to the making of a person who was more knowledgeable of the world. In these terms, internal migration served to increase symbolic capital, whereas international migration would do the opposite in the view of many who were in a position to get by in Ethiopia. While Liechty (2012) suggests that class is becoming increasingly transnational, Lentz (2020) questions the extent to which migrants can convert educational achievements and material resources acquired abroad into status 'back home,' pointing out that there are different reference groups for status. These differences point to why urban-to-urban migration became a preferred choice for some, and that it was a pattern that enabled them to increase their status in ways that meant progress to them.

Thus, those who engaged in migration between urban centres had their own view of what constituted progress, and this differed from that of people who engaged in other forms of migration or who chose to stay put. This provides an initial sense of how this kind of migration contributed to shape a group of people who were transformed through their movements and association with developed cities, interactions with people from diverse backgrounds and new knowledge of the world. Next, I turn to the role of higher education in shaping commonalities in turns of experience, employment trajectories and financial situations.

References

Abbink, Jon. 2012. "Dam Controversies: Contested Governance and Developmental Discourse on the Ethiopian Omo River Dam." *Social Anthropology* 20 (2): 125–44.

———. 2017. *A Decade of Ethiopia: Politics, Economy and Society, 2004–2016*. A Decade of ... Series. Leiden and Boston: Brill.

Admassie, Yeraswork. 2008. "The Gated Communities of Inner-City Addis Ababa." *Journal of Ethiopian Studies* 41 (1–2): 111–41.

Andersson, Ruben. 2014. *Illegality, Inc.: Clandestine Migration and the Business of Bordering Europe*. Oakland: University of California Press.
Atnafu, Adamnesh, Linda Oucho, and Benjamin Zeitlyn. 2014. "Poverty, Youth and Rural-Urban Migration in Ethiopia." Migrating out of Poverty Research Programme Consortium, Working Paper 17. University of Sussex.
Bezu, Sosina, and Stein Holden. 2014. "Are Rural Youth in Ethiopia Abandoning Agriculture?" *World Development* 64 (December): 259–72. https://doi.org/10.1016/j.worlddev.2014.06.013.
Blerk, Lorraine van. 2008. "Poverty, Migration and Sex Work: Youth Transitions in Ethiopia." *Area* 40 (2): 245–53.
Bonsa, Shimelis. 2013. "City as Nation: Imagining and Practicing Addis Ababa as a Modern and National Space." *Northeast African Studies* 13 (1): 167–213.
Bulcha, Mekuria. 1988. *Flight and Integration: Causes of Mass Exodus from Ethiopia and Problems of Integration in the Sudan*. Uppsala: Scandinavian Institute of African Studies.
Clapham, Christopher. 2006. "Ethiopian Development: The Politics of Emulation." *Commonwealth & Comparative Politics* 44 (1): 137–50.
———. 2018. "The Ethiopian Developmental State." *Third World Quarterly* 39 (6): 1151–65. https://doi.org/10.1080/01436597.2017.1328982.
CSA. 2007. "The 2007 Population and Housing Census of Ethiopia: Statistical Report for Addis Ababa City Administration." Addis Ababa, Ethiopia: Central Statistics Agency.
———. 2012. "The 2010/2011 Ethiopian Households Consumption—Expenditure (HCE) Survey." Addis Ababa, Ethiopia: Central Statistical Agency.
De Haas, Hein. 2007. "Turning the Tide? Why Development Will Not Stop Migration." *Development and Change* 38 (5): 819–41.
De Neve, Geert. 2003. "Expectations and Rewards of Modernity: Commitment and Mobility Among Rural Migrants in Tirupur, Tamil Nadu." *Contributions to Indian Sociology* 37 (1–2): 251–80.
Di Nunzio, Marco. 2019. "Not My Job? Architecture, Responsibility, and Justice in a Booming African Metropolis." *Anthropological Quarterly* 92 (2): 375–401. https://doi.org/10.1353/anq.2019.0019.
Donham, Donald L. 1999. *Marxist Modern: An Ethnographic History of the Ethiopian Revolution*. Berkeley: University of California Press.
Dorosh, Paul, and Emily Schmidt. 2010. "The Rural-Urban Transformation in Ethiopia." International Food Policy Research Institute

(IFPRI). https://pdfs.semanticscholar.org/9e64/6f5da7c1f9eb642be3b92a84d7d8e69c49fe.pdf.

Ellison, James. 2009. "Governmentality and the Family: Neoliberal Choices and Emergent Kin Relations in Southern Ethiopia." *American Anthropologist* 111 (1): 81–92.

Erulkar, Annabel S., Tekle-Ab Mekbib, Negussie Simie, and Tsehai Gulema. 2006. "Migration and Vulnerability Among Adolescents in Slum Areas of Addis Ababa, Ethiopia." *Journal of Youth Studies* 9 (3): 361–74.

FDRE. 2002. 'Foreign Affairs and National Security Policy and Strategy'. Addis Ababa: Federal Democratic Republic of Ethiopia, Ministry of Information.

Ferguson, James. 1999. *Expectations of Modernity: Myths and Meanings of Urban Life on the Zambian Copperbelt*. Berkeley: University of California Press.

Fernandez, Bina. 2010. "Cheap and Disposable? The Impact of the Global Economic Crisis on the Migration of Ethiopian Women Domestic Workers to the Gulf." *Gender and Development* 18 (2): 249–62.

French, Matthew, and Kathrine Hegab. 2011. "Condominium Housing in Ethiopia: The Integrated Housing Development Programme." Nairobi: UN Habitat.

Gardner, Katy. 1995. *Global Migrants, Local Lives: Travel and Transformation in Rural Bangladesh*. Oxford: Clarendon Press.

Gebre, Liqu Teshome, Pranitha Maharaj, and Natashya K. Pillay. 2010. "The Experiences of Immigrants in South Africa: A Case Study of Ethiopians in Durban, South Africa." *Urban Forum* 22 (1): 23–35.

Gebresenbet, Fana. 2014. "Securitisation of Development in Ethiopia: The Discourse and Politics of Developmentalism." *Review of African Political Economy* 41 (Supplement 1): S64–74.

Graw, Knut, and Joska Samuli Schielke, eds. 2012. *The Global Horizon: Expectations of Migration in Africa and the Middle East—Google Books*. Leuven University Press.

Hansen, Karen Tranberg. 2005. "Getting Stuck in the Compound: Some Odds against Social Adulthood in Lusaka, Zambia." *Africa Today* 51 (4): 3–16.

Haustein, Jörg, and Terje Østebø. 2011. "EPRDF's Revolutionary Democracy and Religious Plurality: Islam and Christianity in Post-Derg Ethiopia." *Journal of Eastern African Studies* 5 (4): 755–72.

Jayadeva, Sazana. 2018. "'Below English Line': An Ethnographic Exploration of Class and the English Language in Post-Liberalization India." *Modern Asian Studies* 52 (2): 576–608.

Jónsson, Gunvor. 2008. "Migration Aspirations and Immobility in a Malian Soninke Village." Working paper. IMI, Oxford. http://imi.socsci.ox.ac.uk/pdfs/wp/wp-10-08.pdf.

Kibreab, Gaim. 1996. "Eritrean and Ethiopian Urban Refugees in Khartoum: What the Eye Refuses to See." *African Studies Review* 39 (3): 131–78.

Kibret, Fitsum Dechasa. 2014. "Unemployment and Labor Market in Urban Ethiopia: Trends and Current Conditions." *Sociology and Anthropology*, 12.

Lavers, Tom. 2012. "'Land Grab' as Development Strategy? The Political Economy of Agricultural Investment in Ethiopia." *Journal of Peasant Studies* 39 (1): 105–32. https://doi.org/10.1080/03066150.2011.652091.

Lefort, Rene. 2015. "The Ethiopian Economy: The Developmental State vs. the Free Market." In *Understanding Contemporary Ethiopia*, edited by Gérard Prunier and Éloi Ficquet, 357–94. Oxford University Press.

Lentz, Carola. 2020. "Doing Being Middle-Class in the Global South: Comparative Perspectives and Conceptual Challenges." *Africa* 90 (3): 439–69. https://doi.org/10.1017/S0001972020000029.

Levine, Donald N. 2004. "Reconfiguring the Ethiopian Nation in a Global Era." *International Journal of Ethiopian Studies* 1 (2): 1–15.

Liechty, Mark. 2012. "Middle Class Déjà Vu: Conditions of Possibility from Victorian England to Contemporary Kathmandu." In *The Global Middle Classes: Theorizing Through Ethnography*, edited by R Heiman, C Freeman, and Mark Liechty. Santa Fe, NM: School for Advanced Research Press.

Mains, Daniel. 2012. *Hope Is Cut: Youth, Unemployment, and the Future in Urban Ethiopia*. Philadelphia: Temple University Press.

Masquelier, Adeline. 2013. "Teatime: Boredom and the Temporalities of Young Men in Niger." *Africa* 83 (3): 470–91.

McGregor, Joann. 2007. "'Joining the BBC (British Bottom Cleaners)': Zimbabwean Migrants and the UK Care Industry." *Journal of Ethnic and Migration Studies* 33 (5): 801–24. https://doi.org/10.1080/13691830701359249.

Mercer, Claire, and Charlotte Lemanski. 2020. "The Lived Experiences of the African Middle Classes Introduction." *Africa* 90 (3): 429–38. https://doi.org/10.1017/S0001972020000017.

Newell, Sasha. 2012. *The Modernity Bluff: Crime, Consumption, and Citizenship in Côte D'Ivoire*. Chicago and London: University of Chicago Press.

Nieswand, B. 2011. *Theorising Transnational Migration: The Status Paradox of Migration*. New York: Routledge.

Orlowska, Izabela. 2013. "Forging a Nation: The Ethiopian Millennium Celebration and the Multiethnic State." *Nations and Nationalism* 19 (2): 296–316.

Østebø, Terje, and Kjetil Tronvoll. 2020. "Interpreting Contemporary Oromo Politics in Ethiopia: An Ethnographic Approach." *Journal of Eastern African Studies* 0 (0): 1–20. https://doi.org/10.1080/17531055.2020.1796255.

Pankhurst, Richard. 1961. "Menelik and the Foundation of Addis Ababa." *The Journal of African History* 2 (1): 103–17.

Piot, Charles. 2010. *Nostalgia for the Future: West Africa After the Cold War*. Chicago: University of Chicago Press.

Rahmato, Dessalegn. 2011. *Land to Investors: Large-Scale Land Transfers in Ethiopia*. Oxford: African Books Collective.

Regt, Marina de. 2010. "Ways to Come, Ways to Leave: Gender, Mobility, and Il/Legality Among Ethiopian Domestic Workers in Yemen." *Gender and Society* 24 (2): 237–60.

Schewel, Kerilyn. 2015. "Understanding the Aspiration to Stay: A Case Study of Young Adults in Senegal." In International Migration Institute Working Paper Series (Working Paper 107): 1–37.

Schewel, Kerilyn, and Sonja Fransen. 2018. "Formal Education and Migration Aspirations in Ethiopia." *Population and Development Review* 44 (3): 555–87. https://doi.org/10.1111/padr.12159.

Shack, W.A. 1973. "Urban Ethnicity and the Cultural Process of Urbanization in Ethiopia." In *Urban Anthropology: Cross-Cultural Studies of Urbanization*, edited by Aidan Southall, 251–85. London: Oxford University Press.

Tegegne, Atsede Desta, and Marianne Penker. 2016. "Determinants of Rural Out-Migration in Ethiopia: Who Stays and Who Goes?" *Demographic Research* 35 (October): 1011–44. https://doi.org/10.4054/DemRes.2016.35.34.

Triulzi, Alessandro. 2006. "The Past as Contested Terrain: Commemorating New Sites of Memory in War-Torn Ethiopia." In *Violence, Political Culture & Development in Africa*, edited by Kaarsholm, Preben, 122–40. Oxford: James Currey.

Vaughan, Sarah. 2011. "Revolutionary Democratic State-Building: Party, State and People in the EPRDF's Ethiopia." *Journal of Eastern African Studies* 5 (4): 619–40.

Vaughan, Sarah, and Mesfin Gebremichael. 2011. "Rethinking Business and Politics in Ethiopia: The Role of EFFORT, the Endowment Fund for the Rehabilitation of Tigray." Research Report 02. London: Overseas Development Institute.

Viezzoli, Claudio. 1992. "Scenarios of Economic Development in the Beles Valley." In *Resettlement and Rural Development in Ethiopia: Social and Economic Research, Training and Technical Assistance in the Beles Valley*, edited by Paolo Dieci and Claudio Viezzoli, 161–80. Milano: Franco Angeli.

Waal, Alex de. 2013. "The Theory and Practice of Meles Zenawi." *African Affairs* 112 (446): 1–8.

Yan, Hairong. 2008. *New Masters, New Servants: Migration, Development, and Women Workers in China*. Durham and London: Duke University Press.

Young, John. 1997. *Peasant Revolution in Ethiopia: The Tigray People's Liberation Front, 1975–1992*. Cambridge: Cambridge University Press.

Zewde, Bahru. 2002. *Pioneers of Change in Ethiopia: The Reformist Intellectuals of the Early Twentieth Century*. Oxford: James Currey.

———. 2005. "The City Centre: A Shifting Concept in the History of Addis Ababa." In *Urban Africa: Changing Contours of Survival in the City*, edited by AbdouMaliq Simone and Abdelghani Abouhani, 120–37. London and New York: Zed Books.

3

Higher Education and Economic Mobility

From Poverty to Employment

Several of my interlocutors came from poor rural and semi-urban backgrounds but had completed higher education degrees. The massive expansion of Ethiopian higher education and implementation of a cost-sharing programme meant that they did not have to pay fees upfront and that they could live in a dormitory on campus and eat three meals a day. Yet some had struggled to complete their degrees because of challenging conditions on campus, as Petros described:

> I studied anthropology in Gondar, a BA degree. In sum, my experience of Gondar was good, but there were some issues with the food there. Gondar is the worst for university food in Ethiopia. The food situation was very bad. After a while I chose to get 280 birr [$15.10] cash a month from the cost-sharing [scheme] instead of eating in the canteen. It was not enough and my family had to send me money, but they couldn't give me enough. I ate only twice per day, following the 5–11 strategy [*ammest-asserand*, i.e. to eat at 11am and 5pm]. Eating less made it difficult to study, I didn't have any energy and I lost interest. I weighed less than 50

M. R. Breines, *Becoming Middle Class*,
Globalization, Urbanization and Development in Africa,
https://doi.org/10.1007/978-981-16-3537-3_3

> kilos at some point. When I think of Gondar now, I think of hunger. It was three years of famine.

The majority of my research participants who had little money and experienced significant hardship during their studies persevered and completed their degrees. Poverty continued to impact their lives during their studies as they had to get by with the food universities offered or try to find alternative solutions as Petros did. The reason for their persistence was that they considered higher education to be a unique opportunity, one that would improve their prospects for well-paid employment and secure themselves and their families in the future. Historically, higher education in Ethiopia has been elitist (Ottaway 1976), and the current discourse on its transformative power can partly be understood in relation to its long-standing association with wealth and power, as well as the visible success of recent graduates.

Out of the 36 interlocutors (23 men and 13 women) with whom I conducted semi-structured interviews, 26 had pursued higher education. All 26 had migrated to other parts of the country for their education. The majority had completed bachelor's degrees from universities as their highest degrees, and three had degrees from private colleges. Five had obtained master's degrees and three others were studying for their master's (one full-time and two part-time) at the time of my research. Two were studying for doctoral degrees at universities abroad (both spent time in Ethiopia during my fieldwork, one to conduct research and the other to write a thesis). Another four were studying for their bachelor's degrees at the time of my research, two at university and two at private colleges. There were also three people who had dropped out of university.

All my interviewees who had studied at higher education institutions had found employment in relatively well-paid positions and earned higher salaries than those without such qualifications and experiences. Many of the people I engaged with who had limited education did manual labour, domestic work, cared for animals, worked as waiters and waitresses in cafes, bars and restaurants, or as drivers and assistants. In such jobs, salaries ranged from as low as 5,000 [$270] to 15,000 birr [$810] a year. For 2010/2011, the national poverty line in Ethiopia was set at 3,781 birr [$204.20] per capita, and 25.7% of the urban population earned less than this amount annually (Atnafu et al. 2014). Interlocutors who had obtained higher education and became teachers made between 13,000 [$702] and 18,000 birr [$972], whereas those who worked in office jobs, as civil servants, in private businesses, and in universities made between 35,000 [$1,890] and 50,000 birr [$2,700] per year. These differences in income show that a university degree could improve people's financial situation significantly. However, even some of the interlocutors who dropped out were more successful than those who did not go to university at all, suggesting that higher education was an opportunity to build social capital even without the formal qualifications.

Some scholars have portrayed education as a key factor for individuals to increase their human capital, but education has also been seen as a system through which privilege and inequality are reproduced (Bourdieu 1984). The idea that formal education breaks down structural inequalities and creates 'meritocratic springboards for upward mobility' has been challenged, especially since the 1970s (Levinson and Holland 1996, 5). Bourdieu and Passeron (1990) have shown education to primarily be a cultural system for reproducing social distinctions and allocating positions in the social hierarchy. Others have demonstrated that these processes take place from kindergarten up to high school and are continued in higher education (Alon 2009). The reproduction of social hierarchies at different levels of education impacts on pupils' and students' achievements, aspirations and interests, which contributes to making it more common for people from more privileged backgrounds to pursue higher education. Because education systems facilitate the embodiment of distinctions, Bourdieu (1984) suggested that education contributes to sustaining social hierarchies rather than providing an opportunity for upwards social mobility. In his view, education is primarily a means for the elites and upper classes to reproduce cultural capital and to keep lower classes in their place.

Other scholars, however, have suggested that higher education can be a means for upwards social mobility. For people from poor backgrounds, going through and completing higher education can be a way to change their lives. Accessing higher education is often the main obstacle because people living in poverty often lack the capital necessary to complete lower levels of education, but not all who access and succeed in higher education are from privileged backgrounds. Reay et al. (2009) have provided an example of how higher education becomes a path for social mobility for limited numbers of students from working-class backgrounds in an elite university in the United Kingdom, which to some extent complicates narratives of universities as sites of social reproduction of privilege. Furthermore, the value of higher education changes when a higher proportion of the population attend university: it becomes less of a marker of distinction compared to when higher education was exclusive to a small group (Friedman and Savage 2017). These contrasting perspectives suggest that there is not a fixed relationship between higher education and social mobility or reproduction, but that these dynamics depend on historical and contextual formations of class.

Higher Education in Africa

In much of Africa, the historical relationship between higher education and class was shaped by colonialism. After the early, formative phase, the development of bureaucratic states through larger institutions and regularisation of authority required a growing number of educated Africans to work as clerks and in more specialised positions (Lawrance et al. 2006). Such employment required training and in response, new education trajectories were provided. The minority who gained access to and completed higher education in colonial contexts were often employed in the public sector (West 2002). These positions enabled people to pursue new lifestyles and opportunities for upwards social mobility that were very different from the lives of peasants and workers (West 2002), showing how class relations during colonial times were partly shaped by education.

Since independence, an expansion of higher education systems has taken place across Africa. These changes have led to debates about how privilege and inequality shape access to higher education as well as its role in social reproduction and upward mobility. With the opening of many new universities and colleges, student numbers in Africa have increased significantly in recent decades. This has created new compositions of students as more people from 'disadvantaged communities' have been able to pursue higher education (Mhlanga 2013). Some scholars are sceptical that such transformations have taken place and suggest that geography, ethnicity, race, gender and socio-economic background remain central to facilitating individuals' access to higher education (Wiseman and Wolhuter 2013). Personal connections and money are also paramount in securing a place at some institutions (see e.g. Willott 2011), which runs counter to narratives about the role of merit in accessing higher education. Students' capacity to succeed at lower levels of education is often a direct outcome of their cultural capital, which suggests that merit, just like personal connections and money, is closely tied to class background.

Recent socio-economic changes across Africa have influenced the prospects for those who gain access to and complete higher education. Since the early 1990s, neoliberal policies and global capitalism have decreased job opportunities in the public sector. Broader access to higher education, combined with a shortage of jobs, has increased unemployment and underemployment for people with degrees (Bryceson 2002; Ralph 2008). Even if people from poor backgrounds get through higher education, deteriorating employment opportunities have impaired their prospects of experiencing upwards social mobility as those with more connections—more social capital—are in better positions to get the jobs that are available.

The declining prospects for graduates have had serious implications for fulfilling social obligations and following expected life trajectories. In Niger, higher education does not offer the same trajectories for work in the Nigérien administration as it used to in the past (Masquelier 2013). Because students with degrees have expectations of jobs that match their qualifications, it is more difficult for the highly educated to find employment than for those who do not have much formal education and can work as car mechanics, tailors or in other 'low-skilled' jobs (ibid.). These circumstances show that the outcomes of completed university degrees depend on local and national economic trends, but also on how people value higher education in different contexts.

Contemporary Higher Education in Ethiopia

Ethiopia is among the many countries that have expanded their higher education systems over the past decades. The EPRDF government issued a range of policies and strategies to expand the sector to meet Ethiopia's need for highly qualified human resources (Yigezu 2013, 40). At the end of the twentieth century, there were only two universities and seventeen colleges (Saint 2004) and the number of students in higher education was about 44,000 (MoE 1998). A large expansion began in 2000 and now, about two decades later, there are 35 universities and more than 98 private higher education institutions across the country (MoE 2020). The rapid expansion has created new challenges and generated concerns over the quality of education. There has been a shortage of qualified academic staff (Van Deuren et al. 2016), and while enrolment quadrupled between 2000 and 2008/2009, the number of teaching staff barely doubled. Less than 20% of teachers had master's degrees and below 4% had doctorates (Reisberg and Rumbley 2015). The quality of university education has also been influenced by the large increase in student numbers. Overcrowded classrooms, shortage of furniture, ICT and up-to-date books and journals have become the norm (Akalu 2014).

In response to the growing cost of this dizzying expansion of higher education, in its 2003 Higher Education Proclamation, the government introduced a cost-sharing scheme (Gebremeskal 2012). The policy of providing food and lodging for the 0.8% of the population enrolled in higher education, who were often from privileged backgrounds, had claimed around 15% of university budgets and questions had been raised about the fairness of providing such benefits for them (Saint 2004). The rationale for the cost-sharing scheme was to diversify the revenue and support the government's effort to expand access to higher education (Yizengaw 2007). Through cost-sharing students can study at university, live in dormitories and eat their meals on campus without paying upfront, but a graduate tax is imposed to repay part of their education cost (Waweru et al. 2011). Students begin payments within a year of graduation and the full amount must be repaid within fifteen years (FDRE 2003). Some study programmes are exempted from repayment, such as training to be primary, secondary and high-school teachers, but these students then have to serve as teachers for a fixed number of years (Ayalew 2012). Cost-sharing only applies to undergraduate studies, but the expansion of higher education as well as the cost-sharing policy is a major break from the elitist tradition where only a small proportion of the population accessed higher education (Yigezu 2013). While higher education was more attractive in the past because the government covered all expenses, the expansion of the higher education sector and introduction of cost-sharing have enabled people from different socio-economic backgrounds to study and obtain degrees.

Despite the expansion, social differences continue to shape access to higher education. Less than 30% of undergraduate students and barely 10% of graduate students in public institutions are female (Reisberg and Rumbley 2015). Female enrolment is much higher in private higher education institutions, at about 50% (Yimam and Nega 2012). The higher proportion of women at such institutions can be understood in relation to the preference for having female students live at home with their families instead of moving to other parts of the country where they are beyond their family's control and protection (Saint 2004). Students on cost-sharing programmes at public institutions are unable to freely choose their preferred programmes and universities (Van Deuren et al. 2016) because the Ministry of Education admits a representative mix of students from different administrative regions to each campus (Saint 2004). Another alternative for people who fulfil the entrance criteria, but do not meet the targets for government sponsorship or are wealthy enough to cover the expenses themselves, is to pursue higher education through paid programmes, either full-time or following evening and summer classes (Waweru et al. 2011). People from poor backgrounds have limited capacity to choose such options and are therefore more likely to move to other parts of the country for their studies, suggesting that social inequalities continue to influence people's opportunities to study and to choose where to study.

The increasing number of graduates has affected well-educated Ethiopians' opportunities to find suitable employment. Education has been narrativised as a key means of finding work and achieving aspirations in urban Ethiopia for half a century, but many young people currently remain unemployed for extended periods of time because 'at the historical moment when expectations of earning membership in an urban middle class through education were expanding, economic opportunity decreased dramatically' (Mains 2012, 89). For people from middle-class backgrounds, unemployment can work as a temporary strategy because they can rely on elaborate systems of reciprocity to get by until they find suitable employment, whereas people from poor backgrounds are not able to postpone employment and are forced out of necessity to find work for which they are over-qualified (Mains 2012). As such, unemployment is not only related to declining job markets, but also to the social positions of individuals.

Rather than centring on unfulfilled expectations and unemployment, this chapter examines the extent to which higher education in Ethiopia offers valuable returns. To consider how higher education changed my interlocutors' lives, I focus specifically on two young men, Yonas and Tesfay, who originated from rural areas outside Adigrat to unpack how higher education and the surrounding processes of migration led to an increase in their economic capital.

First, I briefly introduce Adigrat to situate Yonas's and Tesfay's backgrounds and lives in their local context.

Adigrat: A Small City in Northern Ethiopia

Over the past 200 years, Adigrat has gradually evolved from farmland located below high mountain peaks to a larger settlement. In the early nineteenth century, Adigrat was not much bigger than its surrounding villages (Isenberg and Krapf 1843; Lindahl 2005), but towards the end of the century, Adigrat's political importance increased as it grew in size and started holding a weekly market. In the build-up to the battle of Adwa in 1896, the Italian army occupied Adigrat and the strategically important mountain ridges surrounding it (Lindahl 2005; Marcus 1994). It was occupied again by Italian invaders from 1936 to 1941 (Mockler 2003). Just a few years later, in 1943, the town was occupied by Tigrayan rebels (Lindahl 2005).

Adigrat kept growing, both in size and in political importance. In the early 1970s, the only high school east of Adwa and north of Mekelle was located in Adigrat (Young 1997). Students from Adigrat at Addis Ababa University supported and influenced the students at Agazi High School, turning it into a local centre for dissent against Haile Selassie's regime and what was perceived by many as Amhara domination. Circumstances deteriorated under the Derg regime, especially from the late 1970s when the civil war intensified. Restrictions upon movement were imposed and private traders could only travel if they paid large bribes, though they still risked being detained or executed. These conditions were strongly felt in Adigrat because of its reliance on trade (Young 1997).

When the civil war ended in 1991 and Eritrea became independent in 1993, people in Adigrat encountered new opportunities for making a living. Much of the trade between Ethiopia and Eritrea passed through the town, leading to a surge in business. Asmara, the capital of Eritrea, is less than 200 kilometres away (Adigrat is located thirty kilometres from the Eritrean border). Labour migration across the border has historically been common for people on both sides of the border (Dessalegn 2004, citing Hammond) and trade in this region has also been a major source of income, both when Eritrea was part of Ethiopia and after its independence.

The relationship between Ethiopia and Eritrea has been crucial for Adigrat, and the 1998–2000 war between the two had major implications on livelihoods in the city. Large-scale forced resettlement of citizens from both countries was implemented and, between 1998 and 2001, almost 95,000 Ethiopians, of whom 70% were Tigrayans, were returned from Eritrea to Ethiopia (Dessalegn 2004). Most of these migrants ended up in urban areas and Adigrat's population of about 50,000 increased dramatically, with the addition of some 37,000 deportees and 10,000 internally displaced persons. This stretched the capacity of schools and health services to the limit and increased urban poverty (ibid.). The conflict also led to a halt in the trade of commodities such as grain and livestock, which had a negative economic impact on many people's lives. With dwindling jobs and income, many young women who faced poverty turned to sex work (ibid.). The border was closed from 1998 (Massa 2020), and was only reopened after peace talks were renewed between Eritrea and Ethiopia in 2018. After several intermittent openings and closings of different border points, the whole border has been closed since early 2019.[1]

At the last census in 2007, Adigrat's population was 57,572 (CSA 2007), and there were about 14,000 households (Gebremariam and Addissie 2014). By 2011/2012 the population was estimated to have grown to 76,447 (World Bank 2015). Currently, Adigrat is not as big as Mekelle (the regional capital, about 120 kilometres to the south), but is larger than the nearby towns of Bizet, Idega Hamus and Sinqata. The city has a hospital and a range of health institutions, bars, photo studios, cafes, restaurants and hotels. Main roads are asphalted and side roads which were once muddy alleys are now cobblestoned streets. Tigrayans form the largest ethnic group. In the Eastern Tigray Zone where Adigrat is located, the total population is 755,343, of which 720,000 are classified as Tigrayan and the second-largest group is Irob with some 28,527 people (CSA 2007). Moreover, there is a steady flow of people from surrounding rural areas, other towns in Tigray as well as Eritrea, entering and settling in Adigrat for shorter or longer periods. Soldiers stationed in the army bases as well as the increasing number of students add to Adigrat's diversity. The population is predominantly Orthodox Christian, though there is also a Muslim neighbourhood and a group of Catholics, each representing about 3% of the town's population.

Since the opening of Adigrat University in 2011, student numbers have increased each year and in 2020 had grown to more than 16,000 regular students and 6,000 students on continuing education programmes (Adigrat University 2020). There are no private higher education institutions and the opportunities for pursuing higher education in Adigrat are limited to those who are allocated a university place there by the government and those who can pay for evening or summer programmes. As elsewhere in Ethiopia, poor people in Adigrat are less likely to turn down offers for university places in other parts of the country through cost-sharing than prospective students from wealthy families who can choose to study where it is convenient for them.

---

[1] There is currently an ongoing war in Tigray and the border between Ethiopia and Eritrea may change through this evolving situation.

Employment opportunities are similar in towns and cities across Tigray. In Adigrat, the main industry is the pharmaceutical factory, and the town's central source of technological expertise, which opened in 1992 and employs more than 500 people. More recently, Adigrat University has become the largest employer, with 1,100 academic staff and the number of support staff expected to reach 1,500 in 2017 (Adigrat University 2016). There are also opportunities for employment in the local government on *qebele* (neighbourhood) and *woreda* (city) levels, as well as in the Eastern Tigray zone administration, which makes it a significant employer for people with higher education degrees. These employment patterns suggest that economic multiplier effects on these sectors have created demand for urban goods and services and stimulated further job creation in private businesses. This has also given rise to employment for people without degrees and from poorer or rural backgrounds: in the marketplace, doing manual labour, in the service sector or as bus, minibus and *bajaj* (rickshaw) drivers.[2]

The cityscape has transformed in ways that reflect these social and economic inequalities. A recent change is that buildings with more than one storey are becoming more common. In 1994, 98.3% of buildings in Ethiopia were single-storied (Abelti et al. 2001), but wealthy investors have since constructed several multi-story buildings and houses in urban centres. In Adigrat, there are a few very large houses and relatively expensive hotels owned by local businessmen or people who have emigrated to the United States or Europe. These contrast to the smaller buildings and stone houses where several people often live together in small rooms (Images 3.1 and 3.2).

The population is growing because of migration from surrounding rural areas as well as Eritrea, but migration out of Adigrat remains an attractive option for some. There are three main roads, which lead south (to Mekelle and Addis Ababa), west (to Aksum, Shire and Sudan) and north (to Eritrea). Migrants going to Europe often travel west to cross the Sudanese border, whereas young men and women heading to the Gulf as

[2] The civil war that started in November 2020 and is still ongoing at the time of writing has changed these circumstances significantly. The pharmaceutical factory and the university have been looted and most economic activities have come to a standstill.

Image 3.1 Construction on a main street, Adigrat

well as people going for higher education or better employment opportunities travel to Mekelle and, often, onwards to Addis Ababa. Mekelle is an attractive option for many as it is the second-largest city after the capital (World Bank 2015), and connectivity has been greatly improved with an asphalted road and frequent minibuses between Adigrat and Mekelle. There are no figures available on migration out of Adigrat specifically, but large numbers of people from the town can be found living in Mekelle as well as in Addis Ababa. This can partly be understood by the fact that these cities are favoured destinations for urban dwellers in Adigrat who seek better opportunities for higher education and employment, and the potential they offer for progress.

Image 3.2 Economic growth and a shifting urban landscape, Adigrat

Yonas: Trekking Guide

The first time I met Yonas, I noticed that he was well-dressed, had expensive shoes, and wore a gold chain around his neck. I often encountered him when walking through Adigrat and when I tagged along with Mehari when he needed to see him to discuss their work. Yonas, 25, was Mehari's colleague and regularly took tourists trekking in the high mountains of Tigray. As we got to know each other better, he told me about his background and work.

As a child, Yonas was sent to live with his grandmother in the countryside outside Adigrat when his father divorced his mother and went away to be a soldier for the TPLF. From first to sixth grade, Yonas attended a local school near his home; in seventh grade, he moved to Agazi High School in Adigrat. In the evenings, Yonas sold cigarettes on the street and slept on the streets because he was afraid to make the long walk to his grandmother's house in the dark. He found shelter with other children on the veranda outside the Red Cross building and was provided regular meals by the organisation. During the war with Eritrea, Yonas started making more money by working as a *delala* (broker) facilitating meetings between sex workers and soldiers. They would each pay him 10 birr [$0.54], enabling him to make 20 birr [$1.08] for each encounter he set up.

Yonas, and many other interlocutors who were born in the final decade of the civil war (which ended in 1991), experienced difficult economic situations during their childhoods. After a few peaceful years, the war with Eritrea (1998–2000) began and fighting took place in close proximity to Adigrat. Schoolchildren like Yonas were sometimes taught in the open air, in places with cover from the artillery shelling behind the mountains south of the city. These circumstances influenced the quality of education and his personal situation added to his difficulties. Nevertheless, Yonas completed secondary school and entered university:

> I studied foreign languages, literature and journalism at Awassa University. I had heard good things about Awassa before going, but I was a bit scared and didn't trust anyone. There were thieves, but nothing happened to me. It was very good to be in Awassa, the city is beautiful and people are nice. The main problem was money, I had 150 birr [$8.10] to live on each month. It took three days to finish it and then I had to borrow from friends. We shared what we had, for example if one guy brought *khat* we all chewed. We lived together.

This generation of students from poor backgrounds who accessed higher education often faced a difficult financial situation during their studies. They struggled even if food and accommodation were arranged through the cost-sharing programme, but most persisted despite different challenges and completed their degrees. In Ethiopia, there is a longstanding narrative that higher education helps in finding employment and fulfilling aspirations (Mains 2012), and in response to this perception, my interlocutors from poor backgrounds developed strategies of reciprocity (see also Tekola 2005) to overcome the difficulties that could hamper their trajectories of expected economic improvement.

After graduating, Yonas returned to Adigrat and was hired as a high-school teacher. The job would pay him about 1,000 birr [$54] a month and was higher than what many people earned in the area where he had grown up outside Adigrat. However, he quit before the job even started: 'I became a research assistant and translator for an Irish MA student. We went to the countryside and did many interviews. I worked with her for five months and she paid 100 birr [$5.40] a day. It was a good salary at that time.' Yonas favoured well-paid short-term employment over a permanent job that paid less. Indeed, many of my interlocutors with higher education degrees were in a position to obtain different kinds of well-paid employment, both in public and private sectors, and could find new employment with less trouble than has been described in case studies from other parts of Africa (Ralph 2008; Masquelier 2013).

When the Irish student finished her fieldwork, Yonas started looking for work again. Through contacts from his student days, it only took him a few weeks before he got a teaching job in Awassa:

> I was happy to go to Awassa. I said goodbye to my family and went to the bus station. I was already waiting for the bus to depart when they called me from the school here in Adigrat and offered me work again. I had to make the choice in the bus and this was a big test for me. The salary is the same in both places and I preferred to be where I have my family and friends so I decided to stay here. It was God's work that I received the call just before leaving. I returned home and my family was surprised to see me again.

His choice to live where he had a stronger social network reflected many interlocutors' preference to live in their place of origin if they had the same employment and income opportunities as in other urban centres. Even if Yonas accounted for his employment history as one of serendipity, it was primarily his higher education degree and expanding networks that provided him with multiple job offers.

He eventually became a teacher in Adigrat, but the job did not live up to his expectations, both in terms of the amount of work it required and its impact on his social life. Because of these unsatisfying conditions, Yonas's career as a teacher was short-lived:

> It's hard to a be a teacher. I was teaching ninth and tenth grade, and there were 65 students in the class. The students make a lot of noise and disturbance; one student shouts, one does this and another something else. I also had to prepare a lot and I had start work very early. When I drank beer at night I thought about my work and my preparations. It was boring. I stopped because I wasn't satisfied with the work and the salary was too small.

People who had obtained higher education and developed expectations of pleasant and well-paid work were sometimes disillusioned. Teaching jobs were considered especially demanding and the income too low to lead the lifestyles my interlocutors aspired for. A common pastime for young men in Adigrat and many other towns in Tigray is to drink beer and try to pick up women. In Uganda, Mills and Ssewakiryanga (2005, 91) find that money was the key symbol through which young men 'imagined, practiced and understood their sexual and social relationships with women.' For Yonas, being a teacher made it impossible to socialise with his male urban peers who had less rigid work hours and earned higher incomes. His work impacted his performance of masculinity and success with women.

These circumstances made him look for other employment. He found a new opportunity after working as a teacher for a short time: 'I saw an advertisement on the road for the job as trekking guide two years ago. I got a recommendation letter from the Irish woman and applied. There was an interview, which I passed, and I got the job.' Yonas's salary was about the same as his teaching job during the first year, but after two years in this position it had increased substantially and he was earning between 3,000 and 8,000 birr [$162–432] a month. Again, Yonas's narrative of shifting employment shows how he chose more profitable and insecure employment over secure, low-paid and unsatisfying work as a teacher. Interlocutors with higher education degrees often aspired to find employment in the private sector, and university degrees and experience of employment in the public sector could be stepping stones to such jobs. In addition to offering higher salaries, there were also better prospects for salary rises and career advancements in the private sector.

Yonas rented a room in a compound in central Adigrat and had a domestic worker who came daily to cook his meals. When he was not working in the mountains or resting at home, he often went out in the evenings to drink and dance with friends, and regularly treated women to dinners and drinks. It was predominantly young, unmarried men in private-sector jobs or from wealthy backgrounds who frequented upmarket venues, whereas people with lower incomes would rarely enter such places. When they did, they often stood out in terms of clothing and behaviour. Yonas's relatively high income enabled him to pursue a lifestyle associated with male urban prosperity, which meant socialising for leisure in the more expensive bars and hotels. Because these urban lifestyles were expensive, those of my interlocutors who experienced economic improvement after higher education often attempted to supplement their income through their own business ventures. Yonas invested some of his surplus in a café to generate a second income. The café was located a bit outside the city centre and I regularly stopped by for tea and a chat with Yonas and the waitress he had hired. There were rarely more than a few customers and after just a few months, he closed it down. While he and many others struggled to generate any profit from their businesses, their capacity to invest in them at all made their financial prosperity more visible in public spaces.

Yonas's financial situation remained stable after his failed business attempt. Still, he kept looking for new and better jobs:

> I applied for a job in Mekelle last summer and had an interview with Fana FM [a radio station], but I didn't get it. Some two weeks ago I received a phone call from a friend I studied with in Awassa who could get me a job as journalist in Mekelle. I wouldn't mind moving to Mekelle because it's in Tigray and life is similar to Adigrat. If I get a good salary I'll go, but what they offered me was only 1,800 birr [$97.20]. Being a trekking guide pays much more and gives me a lot of satisfaction.

Migration was a strategy for seeking better employment opportunities used by several of my interlocutors who had completed higher education. For many people in Adigrat, Mekelle was an attractive city with its many bars, restaurants and cafes, as well as its diversity and more cosmopolitan atmosphere. Yonas had already enhanced his economic situation significantly and moving to a bigger city would not necessarily increase his income. Although he decided to stay in Adigrat, Yonas's consideration of a move to nearby Mekelle, and his capacity to turn down the job offer, illustrates that urban-to-urban migration was a pattern of movement he and others with higher education degrees associated with wider job prospects. Yonas's story shows the potential of higher education to provide employment opportunities to individuals, but also the centrality of migration between cities in these processes. I will explore this further through the case of Tesfay.

Tesfay: Lawyer

In my conversations with Tesfay, 28, it became clear that higher education had been central in improving his economic situation and way of living. Like Yonas, Tesfay experienced poverty in his childhood. He was born to a poor farming family in the mountains outside the town of Bizet, which is located about an hour's travel by car from Adigrat. He had two siblings and his parents were uneducated farmers who struggled to provide for their children. In Tesfay's early childhood, his family temporarily relocated to western Tigray when drought and famine made survival challenging. After returning, Tesfay went on to complete sixth grade in the rural area where he was born, before starting his daily walk of about an hour to and from Bizet to attend seventh and eighth grades. There was no opportunity for further education in Bizet at that time and, aged fifteen, Tesfay moved to Adigrat on his own to continue his studies (Image 3.3).

In Adigrat, Tesfay had very little money. He shared a cheap room with friends and could not afford to eat regularly. Nevertheless, he managed to pass his final exams and obtained good enough grades to access university through the cost-sharing programme. Tesfay got into the law programme at Jimma University in southwestern Ethiopia:

Image 3.3 Mountainous landscape close to Tesfay's village

> It was a big relief for me when I joined the university because they served food three times a day. The food at Jimma University was very nice, especially compared to the food I ate in the countryside. When I was at university I had food and accommodation, so I didn't think about food, about house rent, only about my education. I was really happy there. Many people complain of university life and the food they get served. Some pretend they had a better life before, but around 80% of the students came from rural areas and surely they had worse lives before. For students from rich families it's difficult live in such conditions.

Whereas for Tesfay the food situation at Jimma University resolved many of the problems he had faced earlier in his life, Petros, discussed at the start of this chapter, found himself in a situation where food became a major challenge to completing his studies. Students' practices and attitudes towards shared accommodation and university food could in some cases reveal their backgrounds and social positions, but also depended on the circumstances at each university as these were known to vary significantly. As a university student, Tesfay remained poor even if he had achieved food security. He could not afford to travel to visit his family in Tigray and spent the summer holidays in Addis Ababa where he worked as an assistant for his uncle on board Higer buses which provided cheap intracity transport. He saw this as a valuable experience as well as an opportunity to become familiar with the capital. He was already at that time aspiring to return to live in Addis Ababa in the future.

After obtaining his university degree, Tesfay moved to Wukro, a small town about seventy kilometres from Adigrat in eastern Tigray, to pursue two-and-half years of training to become a prosecutor. Under the cost-sharing programme, he was subsequently sent to work for two years as a prosecutor in Endabugena, western Tigray. The cost-sharing programme not only enabled students from poor backgrounds to go to university, but mandatory placements provided them with employment and income (depending on their discipline). This employment often required migration, and while students who were on study programmes to become teachers were frequently sent to rural areas, those with other degrees were often deployed to cities and towns. This migration for employment across Ethiopia as part of participation in the cost-sharing programme contributed to institutionalise urban-to-urban migration, and familiarised interlocutors with different locations. Their migrations expanded their networks (social capital) and often shaped employment trajectories, and thereby also enhanced their economic capital. When the mandatory placement in Endabugena ended, Tesfay obtained employment as a prosecutor in Wukro, where he made a monthly salary of 3,332 birr [$180] and received a housing allowance of 200 birr [$10.80].

One afternoon in 2013, Mehari and I travelled a bit more than an hour from Adigrat by minibus to visit Tesfay in Wukro. Tesfay met us on the street outside where he lived and invited us into his small room in the compound he shared with several other residents. We sat down on his bed and there was a small TV, and a few cooking utensils, his clothes and a single lightbulb. I noticed that there was a charcoal stove and I asked if he was a good cook. He responded, 'I only use it to make tea in the morning, I eat my meals outside.' Apart from some exceptions, my male interlocutors considered cooking and household chores to be women's work. These gender relations influenced how men lived their lives and performed their masculinity both in private and public spaces, with the result that many unmarried men ate most of their meals in restaurants or engaged female domestic workers to cook for them.

As the sun was setting, we went for a walk along the main road through Wukro. We enjoyed our dinner in a popular restaurant and spent the rest of the evening sitting around a small table on the pavement outside a bar, drinking beers and catching up on work and common friends. Mehari and Tesfay reminisced about their experiences at Jimma University where both had studied. Among those who obtained well-paid employment after higher education, it was common to socialise in restaurants and bars, unlike those with lower incomes and other social networks. Men like Mehari and Tesfay who had pursued higher education and started earning relatively high incomes often led urban lifestyles associated with prosperity and wealth, which included going for tea and coffee at cafés several times a day, regularly having lunch and dinner with colleagues and friends in restaurants, and often spending their evenings drinking beer in bars. Women occasionally participated in these practices, though many maintained their respectability by not socialising outside the household in the evenings. Prices in the places my interlocutors frequented were much higher than the places where people with lower incomes gathered to eat, drink and pass time. For example, the price of a bottled beer in bars popular among those with high incomes was between 12 and 15 birr [$0.65–0.81], whereas people with low incomes often drank local beer (*sewa*) costing a birr [$0.054] a mug.

Whereas Mehari and Tesfay lived comfortable lives, many urban dwellers in Tigray with higher education degrees argued that migration to the capital was the best route to living a fulfilling life. However, living costs in Addis Ababa exceeded what most could afford immediately after graduating. Instead of moving to the capital, most worked in other parts of the country, either to complete the mandatory period of employment for the cost-sharing programme or simply to live in more affordable places. Many migrated to other urban areas in Tigray for employment and for most it was only after their economic situations improved, or if they could draw on support networks offering accommodation and food while seeking employment, that they considered it possible to migrate to Addis Ababa.

In 2014, Tesfay migrated to Addis Ababa and started his own law firm. There, the room Tesfay rented to live in was of a similar standard to the one in Wukro, but he also had a nice office on the fourth floor of a large building with a mix of shops and other businesses in the Megenagna neighbourhood. As he showed me around on my visit, he sat down in his office chair behind the huge desk and pointed to show me his degree certificates on the wall. His capacity to relocate to the capital and take the step from the public to the private sector shows his economic improvement from when he was growing up in rural poverty. This became possible through his higher education and migration trajectory in the preceding years.

Whereas Tesfay had moved between several urban centres, his family remained in rural areas of Tigray. This made their lives very different: 'My father lives in Bizet. I have no mother, she died around the time I graduated. My brother and sister are farmers. My sister lives in the countryside an hour's walk from Bizet and my brother lives in the countryside outside Shire.' Through his account of his family's livelihoods, Tesfay illuminated the differences in their lives and what would have been a more likely life for him if he had not completed school and gone to university. These differences became even clearer to me on one occasion, when Tesfay, Mehari and I took a minibus from Adigrat to visit Tesfay's father in Bizet. After arriving, we walked to the house of a relative of Tesfay where his father was waiting for him. He had walked down from his village earlier in the day and was sitting outside in the shade. Looking at Tesfay and his father who was dressed in worn clothes and a *shamma* (white cotton shawl) that had seen better days, it was clear that they lived very dissimilar lives, both in terms of the environments they were living in and their livelihoods. There was an economic gap between interlocutors who came from poor, rural backgrounds and completed higher education, and their families who often continued to live in poverty. Most supported their families financially, but these variations within families call into question conventional approaches to class, which consider families as belonging to the same group (Lentz 2020).

Tesfay's story points to how higher education and migration between urban centres could improve individuals' economic situations, which is in contrast to the more common narratives of marginalisation and failures of development among people who stay in one city (see e.g. Di Nunzio 2019). Upward social mobility is often supported by work in different sectors (Lentz 2020), though for Tesfay and others I engaged with, it was the multiple stints of migration for study and work that were central in changing livelihoods and social position.

Higher Education as Transformative

Opportunities to study at university remain unequal in Africa (Wiseman and Wolhuter 2013) regardless of the expansion of higher education systems in many countries. People's chances of completing lower levels of education are embedded in broader patterns of privilege and inequality (Willott 2011; Woldehanna and Hagos 2015; Poluha 2007); however, there are also growing numbers of people from poor backgrounds who access and complete higher education in Ethiopia. Social inequalities continue to shape higher education trajectories, exemplified by the difficulties some students face in getting by on the cost-sharing programme, but if they manage to get past these challenges the degrees have the potential to improve their lives. These opportunities primarily exist in or close to urban centres and large numbers of young people aspire to migrate within the country to continue their education and obtain professional work (Schewel and Fransen 2018).

Yonas's and Tesfay's stories highlight how the expansion of higher education has generated access to university studies for people from poor backgrounds. Despite the inflation of educational credentials around the world (Parker 2013), education is for many people the most certain means of improving access to better-paid employment (Lentz 2020). Yonas came from a poor background and, being a *godana tedadari* (someone who sleeps on the street), his circumstances were not favourable for completing lower levels of education, let alone accessing higher education. Tesfay lived on his own from a young age and experienced food shortages which were disadvantageous for studying. Many children in Ethiopia who face similar conditions drop out before finishing their education (Poluha 2007; Admassu 2011). As their trajectories show, both lower levels of education and higher education continue to reproduce aspects of privilege and inequality, but there are also opportunities for people from poor backgrounds who complete higher education to obtain well-paid employment.

The employment trajectories and economic improvement available to those who entered higher education suggest that wider access to higher education has enabled those who gain access to university education to increase their economic capital. Both Tesfay and Yonas began pursuing lifestyles associated with urban prosperity, such as spending time in restaurants and bars. They dressed well and distinguished themselves from those who lived in poverty. Whereas poor people with low incomes had limited clothing, often with holes and other signs of wear and tear, and rarely more than one pair of shoes, male interlocutors who earned well could afford to expand their wardrobes and own several shirts, jeans, trousers and pairs of shoes, which enabled them to perform a distinct form of masculinity and sexual confidence determined by their visible wealth (Mills and Ssewakiryanga 2005). While such shifts in lifestyles demonstrate economic improvement, Yonas's attempt to run a café and Tesfay's establishment of a law firm in the capital exemplify how people attempted to invest their economic surplus to yield further income. In addition to the potential such businesses offered for income, being the person in charge made their material wealth and shifting social position more visible.

All my interlocutors who had been to university had migrated to other urban centres to study, but this was also a common strategy for finding better employment after completing higher education. Indeed, it was more common for my interlocutors to migrate for employment and higher salaries in other urban centres than to stay in their place of origin as Yonas did. Even though Yonas was able to obtain well-paid employment and chose to live in Adigrat, migration remained an option for him, both when he was jobless in Adigrat and when he was looking for better alternatives to his current position. Tesfay, on the other hand, moved between several towns in Tigray before migrating to Addis Ababa. Their trajectories of migration differed, but both stories show that urban-to-urban migration for higher education was key for people to transform their lives. Such transformations often led to further migration and points to the relationship between migration and the formation of commonalities between these migrants.

The value of higher education in Africa has changed through its recent expansion. Anthropologists have pointed out that educated young men struggle to obtain employment suitable to their levels of education (Masquelier 2013; Mains 2012) but the experiences of my interlocutors demonstrate that some were in fact able to find well-paid employment suitable to their qualifications—even if they sometimes chose not to take it, like Yonas who turned down the job offer in Mekelle. This suggests that the expansion of higher education in Ethiopia has generated new avenues for some to improve their livelihoods and my interlocutors valued higher education highly because it helped them enhance their income and pursue modern lifestyles. Bourdieu and Passeron (1990) argued that even if education could enhance individuals' incomes, it is unlikely that people from poor backgrounds can cross cultural boundaries and experience social mobility. In their terms, education reproduces social hierarchies. In Ethiopia, higher education enabled my interlocutors to find employment and good incomes, which was, for them, a major improvement from the circumstances in which they grew up. These dynamics point to an important aspect of middle-class formation, and I turn next to the status implications to further explore the role of higher education in class relations.

References

Abelti, Gebeyehu, Marco Brazzoduro, and Behailu Gebremedhin. 2001. "Housing Conditions and Demand for Housing in Urban Ethiopia." Central Statistical Authority; Institute for Population Research—National Research Council (Irp-Cnr). Italian Multi-Bi Research Project ETH/92/P01. Addis Ababa, Ethiopia; Roma, Italy.

Adigrat University. 2016. "About Us." Adigrat University. http://www.adu.edu.et/about-us/.

———. 2020. "About Us ." Adigrat University. http://www.adu.edu.et/about/.
Admassu, Kassahun A. 2011. "Primary School Enrollment and Dropout in Ethiopia: Household and School Factors." In *Proceedings from Population Association of America 2011 Annual Meeting*, 1–42. Washington DC, USA: Princeton University.
Akalu, Girmaw Abebe. 2014. "Higher Education in Ethiopia: Expansion, Quality Assurance and Institutional Autonomy." *Higher Education Quarterly* 68 (4): 394–415.
Alon, Sigal. 2009. "The Evolution of Class Inequality in Higher Education: Competition, Exclusion, and Adaptation." *American Sociological Review* 74 (5): 731–55.
Atnafu, Adamnesh, Linda Oucho, and Benjamin Zeitlyn. 2014. "Poverty, Youth and Rural-Urban Migration in Ethiopia." Migrating Out of Poverty Research Programme Consortium, Working Paper 17. University of Sussex.
Ayalew, Sewale Abate. 2012. "Financing Higher Education in Ethiopia: Analysis of Cost-Sharing Policy and Its Implementation." *Higher Education Policy* 26 (1): 109–126 (Retraction published 11 June 2013).
Bourdieu, Pierre. 1984. *Distinction: A Social Critique of the Judgment of Taste*. Translated by R. Nice. Cambridge, MA: Harvard University Press.
Bourdieu, Pierre, and Jean-Claude. Passeron. 1990. *Reproduction in Education, Society and Culture*. London: Sage.
Bryceson, Deborah Fahy. 2002. "Multiplex Livelihoods in Rural Africa: Recasting the Terms and Conditions of Gainful Employment." *The Journal of Modern African Studies* 40 (1): 1–28.
CSA. 2007. *The 2007 Population and Housing Census of Ethiopia: Statistical Report for Tigray Region*. Addis Ababa, Ethiopia: Central Statistics Agency.
Dessalegn, Bezaiet. 2004. "Ethiopia." Folder. Ethiopia—Forced Migration Online. http://www.forcedmigration.org/research-resources/expert-guides/ethiopia/alldocuments.
Di Nunzio, Marco. 2019. *The Act of Living: Street Life, Marginality, and Development in Urban Ethiopia*. Cornell University Press.
FDRE. 2003. "Council of Ministers Higher Education Cost-Sharing, Regulation No. 91/2003." Addis Ababa: Federal Democratic Republic of Ethiopia, Negarit Gazeta.
Friedman, Sam, and Mike Savage. 2017. "Time, Accumulation and Trajectory: Bourdieu and Social Mobility." In *Social Mobility for the 21st Century: Everyone a Winner?*, edited by Steph Lawler and Geoff Payne, 1st ed., 67–79. 1 Edition. | New York : Routledge. https://doi.org/10.4324/9781351996808.

Gebremariam, Alem, and Adamu Addissie. 2014. "Intention to Use Long Acting and Permanent Contraceptive Methods and Factors Affecting It Among Married Women in Adigrat Town, Tigray, Northern Ethiopia." *Reproductive Health* 11 (1): 24.

Gebremeskal, Tilahun Gidey. 2012. "Governance Arrangement in the Ethiopian Higher Education System—Moving Towards Quasi-Market?" *Ethiopian Journal of Education and Sciences* 7 (2): 33–41.

Isenberg, C.W., and J.L. Krapf. 1843. *Journals of the Rev. Messrs. Isenberg and Krapf: Missionaries of the Church Missionary Society*. London: Seeley, Burnside, and Seeley.

Lawrance, Benjamin Nicholas, Emily Lynn Osborn, and Richard L. Roberts. 2006. "Introduction: African Intermediaries and the 'Bargain' of Collaboration." In *Intermediaries, Interpreters, and Clerks: African Employees in the Making of Colonial Africa*, edited by Benjamin N. Lawrance, Emily Lynn Osborn, and Richard L. Roberts, 3–34. Madison: University of Wisconsin Press.

Lentz, Carola. 2020. "Doing Being Middle-Class in the Global South: Comparative Perspectives and Conceptual Challenges." *Africa* 90 (3): 439–69. https://doi.org/10.1017/S0001972020000029.

Levinson, Bradley A., and Dorothy C. Holland. 1996. "The Cultural Production of the Educated Person: An Introduction." In *Cultural Production of the Educated Person: Critical Ethnographies of Schooling and Local Practice*, edited by Bradley A. Levinson, Douglas E. Foley, and Dorothy C. Holland, 1–54. Albany, NY: State University of New York Press.

Lindahl, Bernhard. 2005. "Local History in Ethiopia." The Nordic Africa Institute. http://www.nai.uu.se/library/resources/dossiers/local_history_of_ethiopia/.

Mains, Daniel. 2012. *Hope Is Cut: Youth, Unemployment, and the Future in Urban Ethiopia*. Philadelphia: Temple University Press.

Marcus, Harold G. 1994. *A History of Ethiopia*. Berkeley: University of California Press.

Massa, Aurora. 2020. "Borders and Boundaries as Resources for Mobility. Multiple Regimes of Mobility and Incoherent Trajectories on the Ethiopian-Eritrean Border." *Geoforum* 116, 262–71, 0016–7185. https://doi.org/10.1016/j.geoforum.2018.01.007.

Masquelier, Adeline. 2013. "Teatime: Boredom and the Temporalities of Young Men in Niger." *Africa* 83 (3): 470–91.

Mhlanga, Ephraim. 2013. *Quality Assurance in Higher Education in Southern Africa: Challenges and Opportunities*. Oxford: Peter Lang.

Mills, David, and Richard Ssewakiryanga. 2005. "'No Romance Without Finance': Commodities, Masculinities & Relationships Amongst Kampalan Students." In *Readings in Gender in Africa*, edited by Andrea Cornwall, 90–95. London: The International African Institute.

Mockler, Anthony. 2003. *Haile Selassie's War*. Oxford: Signal Books.

MoE. 1998. *Education Statistics Annual Abstract 1996/97*. Addis Ababa: Ministry of Education.

———. 2020. "Higher Education Sub-Sector—FDRE Ministry of Education." 2020. http://www.moe.gov.et/web/guest/higher-education-admission.

Ottaway, M. 1976. "Social Classes and Corporate Interests in the Ethiopian Revolution." *The Journal of Modern African Studies* 14 (3): 469–86.

Parker, David S. 2013. "Introduction: The Making and Endless Remaking of the Middle Class." In *Latin America's Middle Class: Unsettled Debates and New Histories*, edited by David S. Parker and Louise E. Walker, 1–22. Lanham, MD: Lexington Books.

Poluha, Eva. 2007. *The World of Girls and Boys in Rural and Urban Ethiopia*. Addis Abeba, Ethiopia: FSS, Forum for Social Studies.

Ralph, M. 2008. "Killing Time." *Social Text* 26 (4): 1–29.

Reay, D., G. Crozier, and J. Clayton. 2009. "'Strangers in Paradise'?: Working-Class Students in Elite Universities." *Sociology* 43 (6): 1103–21.

Reisberg, Liz, and Laura Rumbley. 2015. "Ethiopia: The Dilemmas of Expansion." *International Higher Education* 58: 23–24.

Saint, William. 2004. "Higher Education in Ethiopia: The Vision and Its Challenges." *Journal of Higher Education in Africa/Revue de l'enseignement Supérieur En Afrique* 2 (3): 83–113.

Schewel, Kerilyn, and Sonja Fransen. 2018. "Formal Education and Migration Aspirations in Ethiopia." *Population and Development Review* 44 (3): 555–87. https://doi.org/10.1111/padr.12159.

Tekola, Bethlehem. 2005. *Poverty and the Social Context of Sex Work in Addis Ababa: An Anthropological Perspective*. Addis Ababa: Forum for Social Studies.

Van Deuren, Rita, Tsegazeab Kahsu, Seid Mohammed, and Wondimu Woldie. 2016. "Ethiopian New Public Universities: Achievements, Challenges and Illustrative Case Studies." *Quality Assurance in Education* 24 (2): 158–72.

Waweru, Kennedy M., Sewale Abate, Guyo H. Huka, and Shano M. Dawe. 2011. "Financing Higher Education in Africa: A Case of Ethiopia Public Universities Cost Containment Measures." *Educational Research* 2 (4): 1089–93.

West, Michael O. 2002. *The Rise of an African Middle Class: Colonial Zimbabwe, 1898–1965*. Bloomington: Indiana University Press.

Willott, Chris. 2011. "'Get to the Bridge and I Will Help You to Cross': Merit, Personal Connections and Money in Access to Nigerian Higher Education." *Africa Spectrum* 46 (1): 85–108.

Wiseman, Alexander W., and Charl C. Wolhuter. 2013. "The Incalculable Promise of the African Continent: Higher Education Rising to the Occasion?" In *The Development of Higher Education in Africa: Prospects and Challenges*, edited by Alexander W. Wiseman and Charl C. Wolhuter, 3–19. Bingley, UK: Emerald.

Woldehanna, Tassew, and Adiam Hagos. 2015. "Economic Shocks and Children's Dropout from Primary School: Implications for Education Policy in Ethiopia." *Africa Education Review* 12 (1): 28–47.

World Bank. 2015. "Ethiopia Urbanization Review." World Bank Group & Cities Alliance. http://documents1.worldbank.org/curated/en/543201468000586809/pdf/100238-WP-EUR-Box393221B-PUBLIC.pdf.

Yigezu, Moges. 2013. "Funding Higher Education in Ethiopia: Modalities, Challenges, Opportunities and Prospects." In *Funding Higher Education in Sub-Saharan Africa*, edited by Damtew Teferra, 38–70. London, UK: Palgrave Macmillan. https://doi.org/10.1057/9781137345783_3.

Yimam, Wossenu, and Mulu Nega. 2012. *Current Issues in Ethiopian Private Higher Education Institutions: Opportunities and Challenges*. Oxford: African Books Collective.

Yizengaw, Teshome. 2007. *The Ethiopian Higher Education: Creating Space for Reform*. Addis Ababa: St. Mary's University College Printing Press.

Young, John. 1997. *Peasant Revolution in Ethiopia: The Tigray People's Liberation Front, 1975–1992*. Cambridge: Cambridge University Press.

4

Being Educated

An Educated Person

It would take more than half an hour to get water boiling on the electric hotplate, the stereo stopped working and the lightbulb hanging from the ceiling hardly gave any light at all in the evenings. After hoping for improvement for weeks, Mehari and I went to the electric corporation next to the bus station to see if the problem could be solved. Mehari asked several people, including the guard outside the building who asked us what our business was and searched us before letting us in, for the right office, before we eventually got hold of the right person. He listened briefly to Mehari's explanation before telling us that the high usage of electricity for food preparation in Adigrat during the holiday a few days earlier had caused a transformer to break down and that this was the reason for our troubles. Mehari explained politely that these conditions had lasted for more than a month in his room and were therefore not related to the holiday. The man asked in a condescending tone why Mehari had not come before and said that such behaviour could be expected of people from rural areas, but not from someone like him.

M. R. Breines, *Becoming Middle Class*, Globalization, Urbanization and Development in Africa, https://doi.org/10.1007/978-981-16-3537-3_4

Mehari told him, still in a polite tone, that he had been busy with work and spent much time out of town. Following some further discussion, the man promised to send an electrician the same evening. As we walked out of the building, Mehari said to me:

> That son of a bitch. Instead of acknowledging that the electric supply is in a poor condition he insults me for not having come before. He tried to divert my attention from them not doing their job. How rude! [*balege*]. If he talks to me like that, how do you think he treats humble farmers who respect authorities?

I knew Mehari was quick-tempered and always ready to respond with an insult, but in this case, he had maintained a more respectful tone than he did in many other situations. Even though Mehari was seen as an urban, educated person (*yetemare saw*) by the official, Mehari knew that the electricity would not be repaired if he did not speak respectfully to him. Status was a factor in encounters with government officials, and well-educated people from the city would be treated more respectfully than 'simple,' uneducated farmers. This was not only the case in government offices as many urban dwellers thought of farmers as simpler people than themselves, and would sometimes refer to someone as a *fara* (country bumpkin) if they said or did something foolish. This word was used to suggest that the person was just like the simple-minded people from rural areas, rather than having the knowledge and wit of urban dwellers who were educated or *arada* (street smart) (see also Di Nunzio 2019). My interlocutors' university studies and their subsequent relatively high incomes changed their social relations. This chapter examines the social practices and status transformations that emerged out of higher education.

Higher Education and Social Mobility

On certain days, graduating students can be seen in their gowns posing for pictures with families, friends and other students on university campuses around Ethiopia, and celebrating their achievements in restaurants and other public places. Pictures from these events are often posted on Facebook where they get many 'likes' and congratulatory comments. The liminal spaces of these rituals of completed higher education are celebrations of students' achievements and mark the transition into what is hoped—or expected—to be a prosperous future. As such performances of students' newfound human capital suggest, completed higher education degrees are highly valued.

Until 'Western' higher education became available in Ethiopia, church education had been the primary form of institutionalised education and had justified and reproduced the political legitimacy of rulers for centuries (Milkias 2008). This began to shift in 1950 when Trinity College opened with 21 students and nine teachers (the name was changed to the University College of Addis Ababa later the same year) (Wagaw 1990). The college gradually expanded and established faculties of arts and science, engineering and building colleges, and branches for agriculture in Dire Dawa and public health in Gondar (Semela 2011). In 1961, it was renamed Haile Selassie I University and further expansion took place, adding faculties of education, law, and medicine, a school of social work, and a college of business administration (ibid.). In the mid-1960s, most students at the university came from urban families of 'traders, clerks, policemen, lower-level government employees – in other words, the Ethiopian petty bourgeoisie' (Ottaway 1976, 475). With about 10,000 undergraduates in 1973 (Balsvik 2005), the higher education system was fully financed by the government, giving students access to free education, health care, accommodation, meals and in some cases allowances to cover living expenses (Wagaw 1990).

Even with these favourable conditions, students became increasingly disgruntled with the monarchy. With independence movements flourishing across Africa in the late 1950s and 1960s, students became increasingly aware that people in Ethiopia were not better off than in formerly colonised nations—indeed, conditions were often worse (Levine 1965). The widening access to education during Haile Selassie's rule made it untenable to keep people in a feudal system (Milkias 2008, 94), and student protests against inequality erupted. Inspired by the Marxist ideology spreading across the world in the 1960s and 1970s, university students helped initiate the revolution that led to the end of Haile Selassie's rule in 1974 (Donham 1992).

To mark the shift away from the monarchy, the Derg regime changed the name of Haile Selassie I University to Addis Ababa University in 1974 (Wagaw 1990). This change did not dispose of pre-existing hierarchical relations: selection into higher education continued to be determined mainly by family background (Krishnan 1996). It also continued to be fully financed by the government (Waweru et al. 2011). The Derg prohibited entrepreneurial educational activities and between 1974 and 1991 there were no private higher education institutions (Akalu 2014). The expansion of higher education was limited to the opening of Ethiopia's second university, Alameya University, in 1985 (Ashcroft and Rayner 2012). It was not until the EPRDF regime that access to higher education began to be expanded, first with the opening of new universities, and then with the introduction of the cost-sharing scheme in the early 2000s. Together these created enough university places to accommodate a number of students from non-elite backgrounds, and provided an avenue for them to enrol despite limited means.

There has been a rapid expansion of higher education in the first two decades of the twenty-first century, but people's social backgrounds continue to shape their opportunities of completing lower levels of education and pursuing higher education. In 2015, the enrolment rate in primary education was around 81% for girls and almost 88% for boys (UNESCO 2020); however, the dropout rate has been estimated to be around 13% (Woldehanna and Hagos 2015). In urban areas, the costs, accessibility of schools and parents' educational background play a role in school attendance (Poluha 2007), and in the country more broadly, circumstances such as a sick adult in the household or the death of a parent, food insecurity and harvest failure have been found to decrease enrolment of children of school-going age (Admassu 2011; Chaudhury et al. 2006).

Lower levels of education are provided for free, but families have to cover the cost of educational materials and school uniforms (Woldehanna and Hagos 2015). An example of how social position influences school attendance has been provided by Heinonen (2013) who found that members of youth gangs and street children in Addis Ababa were unlikely to complete lower levels of education because many had to earn a living, faced ill-treatment by teachers and saw only limited job opportunities for those who completed education. Clearly, children in such positions are unlikely to go on to enter higher education. On the other hand, children from families who could afford the expensive, high-quality private primary and secondary schools that have opened since the early 2000s are more likely to advance to university than students who attend government schools (Mains 2012, 5). As such, people from wealthier backgrounds are in a comparatively advantaged position to access higher education because their lower education is at better schools and they can choose where to go to university or pay for private higher education.

Still, it is not only economic capital that determines access to higher education. Bourdieu (1984) considered education a central factor in restraining upward class mobility for the poor and a means for the elites to stay in their powerful positions. Other scholars have explored other forms of social reproduction through education, such as how economic privilege is reproduced (Apple 1982), how working-class distinctions are shaped (Willis 1977) and how education reinforces gender roles and the subordination of women (Delamont 1989; Weiler 1988). While these dynamics are embedded in local contexts and are slowly changing over time, the debates about the role of education in reproducing privilege illustrate that the outcomes of higher education are embedded in a range of social relations.

Migration is often at the intersection between higher education and upward social mobility. This has primarily been explored through the growing field of international student migration (King and Raghuram 2013). This form of migration has increased significantly across the world (Riaño et al. 2018), which has led to studies of, among other topics, students' experiences abroad (Waters and Brooks 2011) and the value of completed international degrees upon return (Collins et al. 2017). Many of these studies have focused on international migration to Western Europe, North America and Australia, whereas in Africa the relationship between higher education and migration is often analysed in terms of 'brain drain,' referring to people with degrees who migrate to other parts of the world (Kritz 2015). Such migrations by highly skilled workers are also common within Africa (Adepoju 2000). The changes in status among those who engage in international or internal migration for higher education, both at their destinations and upon return, remain largely unexplored in the context of Africa. In Ethiopia, the expansion of higher education over the past two decades, combined with the policy of mixing students from different regions, has increased internal migration.

Being a Student

The introduction of cost-sharing, along with the expansion of universities and private education institutions in Ethiopia starting in the early 2000s, has expanded access to higher education and made it less elitist. There are still obstacles for people from poor backgrounds to access higher education, and the need for them to migrate to other parts of the country adds to their difficulties in completing degrees. For many, going to university is the first time they leave their parents' home for an extended period. Some of my interlocutors found this to be an exciting opportunity, like Mehari who went to Jimma University at the age of eighteen:

> It was my first time to leave home. I had not been to another region in Ethiopia before that, only to Mekelle a few times. I was very happy to go to Jimma because life here was like prison until I finished grade twelve. All the time work, work, work for the family. I was happy to go to a place far away, to see Addis Ababa and Jimma.

During his childhood, Mehari had spent a lot of time looking after cattle outside Adigrat and doing household chores which he had found boring. He frequently referred to his father as *tankara* (strong, powerful) because of how he had used violence to control Mehari (and his siblings) as a child. Like other interlocutors who grew up in families where they had to work hard to contribute to their households, Mehari wanted to live his life free from controlling parents and relatives. By moving to another part of the country for his university studies he, like many others, began shifting from being subordinate children to becoming independent adults, and thereby also transforming their positions within their families.

The ways in which university education influenced family relations depended on social origin. Solomon, a 24-year-old university student in Addis Ababa, who was originally from the Benishangul-Gumuz region bordering Sudan, expressed his sense of duty to complete his degree and earn a salary:

> *Solomon*: My father is dead, and the rest of my family live in the countryside and work as farmers. I'm the only one who has left to study and this gives me a lot of responsibility. I have to support my family.
> *Markus*: How is your family? Are you in touch with them?
> *Solomon*: I haven't had any contact with my family since I came here, there is no way of communicating. Anything could have happened while I've been away.

Going to university generated new social dynamics and, in some cases, responsibilities. Moving to a city for university studies often changed my interlocutors' tastes, aspirations and consumption patterns into a distinct but shared set of ideas, and such individual transformations also influenced their positions within families and as men and women. Whereas Mehari had experienced his university studies as a form of escape and a way of attaining freedom, Solomon's emphasis on his responsibility for his family suggests that social ties persisted over long distances despite little or no means of communication. Their different roles in their families can be traced to their individual backgrounds. Mehari's father was a civil servant and his two elder brothers had already studied at university. He had grown up with some economic security, whereas Solomon's father had died and he was the first in his family to access university. This put him in a unique position, with a lot of pressure to complete his degree, find well-paid employment and improve his family's income.

Migration to other parts of the country and encounters with students from various backgrounds also helped my interlocutors expand their social networks. Abebe, a 26-year-old man, was from a family of jewellers in Bahir Dar, the regional capital of the Amhara region. After completing his bachelor's degree in the social sciences at Addis Ababa University, he found a job as a consultant at an NGO for disabled people. He worked there for almost two years before he went to Europe to study for a master's degree with financial support from his parents. After completing a year of coursework, Abebe returned to Ethiopia in the second year to write his dissertation. While writing, he started a company to import goods from China and spent a lot of time dealing with paperwork, permits and trying to get approval to buy US dollars through state banks. We often met for lunch, but he was frequently late for our appointments because his dealings with the bureaucracy took longer than expected. On one of these occasions, we were talking about when we were both students at Addis Ababa University, and Abebe remarked:

> It was a very good time. I met people from all over Ethiopia and there were also students from Nigeria and South Sudan. I like meeting people from other places because it widens your mind. It was very different from Bahir Dar.

Being a university student enabled Abebe to encounter and interact with people from a wide range of backgrounds. Addis Ababa University has more foreign students than other universities in Ethiopia. There are also foreigners at other universities, such as the Eritrean refugees who are allowed to study and Indian lecturers who are hired because of the lack of local staff with master's and doctoral degrees (Semela 2011). In addition to the interactions with foreigners, the government's policy of sending students to different regions of the country (Ayalew 2012) enabled students to develop relations across ethnic lines and widen their social networks. People who did not go to university and who lived in small cities, especially in the Tigray region, had limited opportunities for meeting foreigners and expanding their networks with Ethiopians from other ethnic backgrounds.

Being a student did not yield status in a predetermined manner: the process of becoming an educated person was negotiated throughout the years of study, both between students and with people off-campus. One evening when both Mehari and I had been busy in different parts of Adigrat, we spoke on the phone and arranged to meet in a restaurant for dinner. When he arrived, he had brought a young woman I had not met before. As we ate, she told me that she had moved from Awassa to Adigrat to study for a bachelor's degree in accounting and that she was living in a dormitory on campus. Before finishing the meal, she had to rush back to campus before the gate closed at 9 pm (if she arrived later, she would not be allowed inside and would have to spend the night elsewhere). Mehari and I stayed in the restaurant. I asked him if he was interested in her, but he said; 'She's spoiled [*molqaqa*]. She told me that she stopped eating on campus after she got typhoid. Other people eat there every day so why can't she?' The mass-produced food on university campuses across the country had a bad reputation, but Mehari's disapproval of her eating outside was also embedded in ideas of how women should behave. Some of my male interlocutors made derogatory comments about women if they were picky or spent time in public places (Image 4.1), and thereby reproduced gendered ideologies of appropriate female behaviours. This recalls Ferguson's (1999) finding that most men

Image 4.1 An outdoor café, Adigrat

were convinced that women were grasping, greedy and selfish creatures who could not be trusted. Being a woman, then, often superseded educational credentials as gender played a more powerful role in many social relations.

In Ethiopia, masculinities are performed in conjunction with a longstanding historical gender ideology of women being inferior to men and marriage practices have often subordinated women (Pankhurst 1992). Such representations of women's conditions do run the risk of representing women as voiceless victims of diverse forms of oppression (Cornwall 2005). However, during the civil war (1974–1991), gender roles shifted. Ethiopian women who fought for the TPLF developed attitudes, skills and identities that were in contrast with existing gender roles (Negewo-Oda and White 2011). When the war ended, however, they were demobilised and many left behind their identities as fighters to readjust to the prevailing gender norms of what it meant to be women in civilian life (ibid.), suggesting that the shift in gender roles during the war was temporary. These shifts in gender relations highlight that both femininities and masculinities are spatially and temporally contingent (Miescher and Lindsay 2003), but also that current masculinities reflect Ethiopia's social history and a gendered ideology wherein male experiences, views and aspirations differ significantly from female social realities. Consequently, the status afforded by completing higher education and possibilities for finding employment are gendered.

Becoming a student changed one's status. Starting university and moving to other parts of the country transformed hierarchical relations within the family, as in the case of Mehari who got a stronger sense of freedom by being away from his family. Students from poorer backgrounds, like Solomon, took on greater responsibility to provide for their families. The unique social compositions on university campuses enabled people like Abebe to expand their networks in ways that were not possible for those who did not go to university. It was therefore both my interlocutors' degrees as well as their experiences as students that contributed to their status in the years that followed because being educated requires more than a demonstration of pre-defined knowledge and is embedded in a wider set of locally valued characteristics and behaviours (Bourdieu 1984).

Shifting Power Relations

After completing higher education degrees and finding employment, many experienced a shift in their social relations. Yonas, the trekking guide encountered in Chapter 3, situated these dynamics in relation to his old job as a teacher in Adigrat: 'I didn't like working as a teacher, but you get to know many people and you get a good name. People respect you as a teacher.' For many people who came from poor, rural backgrounds (Image 4.2), being a teacher was a highly esteemed occupation. Nevertheless, it paid relatively little compared to other professional jobs which required higher education, and the opportunities for further economic improvement were limited. Like Yonas, several of my research participants with higher education degrees worked as teachers for less than a year before moving on to more profitable employment.

Image 4.2 Agricultural work, rural Adigrat

My interlocutors assessed their own progress partly by the kinds of employment they obtained after completing higher education. It was, however, their stable incomes that enabled them to transform their social relationships, as Tesfay, the lawyer who moved to Addis Ababa, explained:

> When I joined the training centre to become a prosecutor in Wukro, it was the first place I started to earn a salary. I could buy everything I needed and pay back my debts. There were many people who helped me in the past, so I had to compensate them. I started to treat the people who did good for me when I was without money.

My interlocutors often used parts of their incomes to treat people, both those they had relied on as well as others who were less financially well off. Tesfay's improved economic situation enabled him to buy other people dinners and drinks in restaurants and bars, give gifts and support acquaintances in need. There was no formal accounting of who paid for another's meals and drinks or gave cash to someone in need, but Tesfay was well aware of who had helped him during the years when he had had little money and had struggled to get by. After completing higher education and obtaining employment, he felt satisfaction in being able to provide for other people, even in cases when it was not an obligation. His newfound capacity to pick up the bill was a social opportunity to convert his economic capital into symbolic capital. From having been reliant on friends and relatives, Tesfay's account of how established social relations were renegotiated through the fulfilment of reciprocal obligations transformed him from being a recipient of others' generosity to being a benefactor, which generated a shift in his relationships with friends and relatives. These often long-standing relations that changed over time again point to the limitations of using income or expenditures to determine class position.

After my interlocutors completed their higher education, their social relations and status shifted. While the kind of employment they obtained, financial situations, family circumstances and other factors made each individual's situation different, they had in common that they did not settle for the status changes they obtained from higher education and by earning stable incomes. Instead, they sought to further enhance both material and symbolic capital by engaging in urban-to-urban migration to find better jobs and establish businesses. For Tesfay, the economic improvement he experienced enabled him to invest and develop his career further. As we shared a pizza in an Addis Ababa shopping mall in 2015, Tesfay opened his wallet and pulled out his newly obtained driver's licence.

Markus: Congratulations! But what will you do with it, are you planning to get a car?
Tesfay: I'm arranging the paperwork for a car now; I'll pick it up next week.
Markus: That's great, but aren't cars very expensive?
Tesfay: It's a very small car, it's about 200,000 birr [$10,800].
Markus: That's a lot of money. What will you use a car for?
Tesfay: I don't really need a car, but it is essential to attract clients. If I have a car it will enhance my reputation as a successful lawyer and I'll get more clients.

Regardless of the condition of a car or other aspects of its owner's living conditions, car owners were commonly spoken of as *habtam* (rich). Cars are classified as luxury items in Ethiopia and are subject to very high taxes, making the price much higher than in Europe. Because of the extraordinarily high prices, cars were clear indications of an individual's financial capacity (Durham 2020). Tesfay's investment in a car not only made his economic prosperity more visible, this conversion of economic capital into symbolic capital also opened new avenues for pursuing further progress.

The new opportunities my interlocutors gained from higher education also gave them more power. Aman had grown up on the outskirts of a small town in the Tigray region, but after completing undergraduate and postgraduate degrees he had obtained employment as a university lecturer in a city outside Addis Ababa. Just as I began my fieldwork, Aman was in the capital. It was only a few days before the funeral of Prime Minister Meles Zenawi in 2012, and the atmosphere in the city was subdued. Mourners gathered in groups and walked through the streets, wailing and carrying beeswax candles. There was a high presence of police throughout the capital, and among the people I had spoken to some were devastated by his death and feared political turmoil or even civil war, whereas others hoped for the end of the Tigrayan-dominated EPRDF government. Aman and I spent a quiet evening as the bars and nightclubs that normally blasted music throughout the night were shut down or only playing instrumental mourning music. The funeral ceremony at Mesqel square was a major event attended by officials from various countries in the continent and beyond, as well as by members of the ruling party and representatives from across the country. I was therefore surprised to learn that Aman had come to Addis Ababa to attend the funeral and asked if it was because he supported the deceased Prime Minister or because he was a member of the EPRDF. My presumption was incorrect: Aman said he was going as a representative of his university, along with a few colleagues. Aman's attendance and association with the elites reveal a major shift in his life from when he grew up in the rural outskirts of a small town. Through his higher education and subsequent university employment, Aman experienced not only economic improvement, but also gained access to events and networks that remained largely unavailable to people with less education and working in less prestigious jobs.

Such changes in employment, status and connections also led to increased power over other people. These dynamics became evident on another occasion Aman came to the capital. His social and economic conditions had improved from when he was growing up, but he was dissatisfied as he did not have much money left after covering the rent and other essentials for his family. He frequently visited Addis Ababa to look for better employment opportunities and we spent the evening in the Piazza neighbourhood, catching up over a few beers. In the bar, there were several men of different ages drinking beer alone, with a few waitresses providing drinks and several scantily dressed women hanging out together, waiting for the evening to get busy. These surroundings reminded me of stories I had recently read in a newspaper about university lecturers using their positions to extort sex from female students by threatening to fail them or promising to give them better grades. I asked Aman if he had heard about such practices, and he said: 'Our salary is very small, only 3,000 birr [$162] a month. This is our only wealth.' For

Aman and many of his peers, their income did not suffice to lead the kind of lives they had expected. I was unable to discern if he was joking and could not bring myself to question him further—partly because I did not want to know.

In Ethiopia, women have been and continue to be subject to power relations skewed in favour of males (Ogato 2013). Men regularly express misogynistic attitudes and behaviours, most commonly manifested in sexual banter and undermining the value of women (see also Ferguson 1999). Whether or not Aman was someone who took advantage of vulnerable female students, his comment pointed to the attainment of both status and power through completed higher education degrees and subsequent employment. Aman's occupation placed him in a position where he could take advantage of students who sought to improve their lives by following a similar trajectory to his. Female students from poor backgrounds who saw university degrees as a unique opportunity to transform their own and their families' lives were vulnerable especially to male university staff who held a great deal of power over students' future livelihoods.

Negotiations of power within universities also impacted on some interlocutors' employment conditions. Daniel had become the head of the sociology department in a university outside Addis Ababa despite being less than thirty years old. His highest educational credential was a master's degree. I wondered how he had obtained such a high position at his age and he made it clear that it was not because of merit:

> The senior staff don't want to do it because there is a lot of paperwork and no benefits to doing the job. That's why they assign someone like me and because I was new, I had to take it. I want to do a PhD in Europe or Canada, but I haven't had time to apply because I have a lot of work.

Those who completed higher education often found relatively well-paid employment that could improve their social positions to some extent, but many were still unable to pursue the lifestyles they had expected to follow from their relatively high-status positions. A title like 'head of department' may be considered a high-ranked position, but in Daniel's case, it hampered opportunities to develop his career, at least temporarily.

Another academic, an associate professor at a university, told me that he had been invited to do a postdoctoral fellowship in the United Kingdom, but that it was impossible for him to take up the offer because he had not yet completed his doctorate. High positions did not necessarily reflect people's qualifications, but they were still of importance in negotiations of status. The increase in material, symbolic and social capital achieved through completed higher education degrees and employment sometimes revealed people's relative lack of cultural capital, which could hamper upwards social mobility. Even so, these changes distinguished such people from those who did not have higher education degrees and had limited chances to increase capital.

Higher education could enhance people's symbolic capital. It enabled Tesfay and Yonas to obtain employment that won them respect, which points to significant change in their lives from when they grew up in poverty. Tesfay's capacity to treat those who had supported him in the past meant that higher education enabled him to obtain and transform economic capital into symbolic capital (Bourdieu 1986). His purchase of a car to attract clients blurred the lines between consumption and investment (see also Kroeker et al. 2018), but also increased his symbolic capital which could subsequently generate more business and, in turn, enhance his economic capital. For Aman, higher education opened up opportunities to participate in important events and gave him power over people in vulnerable situations, whereas Daniel's challenging position at his university points to the paradoxical and sometimes unfulfilling status transformations that can follow higher education. The changes in their lives did not always result in what they had expected, partly because the value of capital differed from place to place.

Migration and 'High' Lifestyles

Many of my interlocutors aspired for prosperity that would enable them to live comfortable lives in urban centres. Higher education degrees and relatively well-paid employment provided this to some extent, but in other cases, migration to bigger cities created new obstacles. Some found that opportunities for upmarket urban lifestyles were not the same everywhere, especially in the capital where the cost of living was higher. Elias captured this when he reflected on his life in Addis Ababa:

> I am a doctor, but what they pay me is not much. It is said that being a doctor is 'high work' [*kefetegna sera*] and that doctors live a high life [*kefetegna hiwot*], but I can't live a high life. I get by and rent a room for myself, but everything is expensive here. Sometimes I work nightshifts in private hospitals to add to my income. Even though I'm fine, I understand that people who can't find work or just work occasionally struggle to get by.

'High work' did not necessarily enable 'high living' in Addis Ababa. In Adigrat, Elias had maintained a comfortable lifestyle on the same salary he earned in Addis Ababa. The cost of living in Addis Ababa made it more difficult for him to lead the kind of life people associated with being educated and a doctor. The idea of high living is different from Bourdieu's (1984) concept of 'high culture' as relating to people's tastes and knowledge of objects and practices, and instead reflects the kind of lifestyle people expected to become available to them through increased economic capital. However, because of the high cost of living in the capital, these lifestyles were not easily accessible even to those who held fixed, high-status employment and income.

The differences between places also had implications for the value of my interlocutors' higher education degrees. After completing a degree in physics at Jimma University, Medhane was sent to teach in a small town south of Shire in Tigray for three years as part of the cost-sharing programme. Having completed his university studies, and working as a teacher, influenced how people saw him there: 'I got respect just for having a degree there.' When his three-year placement ended, he continued in the same job for two more years before moving to Mekelle where he taught at a private school for a year. He subsequently migrated to Addis Ababa where he was hired through a friend as a site manager on a construction site and started taking evening classes studying civil engineering at a private college. Here, Medhane lived in a tiny room and just about managed to get by on his salary: 'Sometimes the monthly salary runs out after two or three weeks, and then I have to ask for 500 birr [$27] from next month's salary. But then it gets difficult the following month again, so it's not easy.' Well-educated migrants also found that the value of their higher education was lower in Addis Ababa: 'No one gives you respect just for having a degree, many people here have been to university,' said Medhane. In other places being educated was enough to gain respect for being among the few people who had been to university. In the capital, he was just one out of many with higher education degrees, which impacted on the opportunities available to him to use his educational background to negotiate his status. Still, even though the value of higher education varied, his degree and social capital enabled Medhane to obtain a much higher position on the construction site than the many uneducated migrant workers from rural areas who ended up doing manual labour. My interlocutors' financial situations in Addis Ababa were somewhat similar, as the cases of Medhane and Elias show, and in many cases 'high living' remained an unfulfilled aspiration.

The inequalities between people were occasionally described in terms of a hierarchy primarily related to people's livelihoods. Amharic terms were used loosely, but resemble how class hierarchies are referred to in English. *Zeqetegna* translates as 'lower' and was often used to refer to the lives of people living in poverty and struggling to get by. All my interlocutors used the middle level, *mekakelegna*, to describe their own lifestyles. This meant that they were not poor and not rich, but had sufficient money to get by and live with some degree of comfort. And, finally, *kefetegna* lifestyles were, as Elias indicated, used to refer to those who lived 'high lives'—a luxurious way of living. While the Amharic terms cast some light on social hierarchies, research on the middle class in Ethiopia needs to go beyond local terminology to develop analytical categories (see also Lentz 2016, 2020) and to analyse the formation of such a group.

People's positions within these hierarchies were not solely related to their possession of economic capital. Several of my interlocutors downplayed international migrants' economic achievements because of their lack of education (as discussed in Chapter 2). Nebay, Mehari's elder brother, was in his mid-thirties and had worked in different jobs while studying part-time at Mekelle University. After he completed his degree in accounting, he had obtained a job in the finance office of Adigrat's local administration. He worked there for seven years before he left this secure position and moved to Mekelle for a new job as a factory manager. After two years, Nebay quit to start his own accountancy business in Adigrat, and built up a network of clients across five cities and towns in Tigray. Nebay travelled frequently between these locations and earned enough to invest in and establish other businesses. He recognised that there were good opportunities for making money abroad, but questioned people who did so:

> Those who go abroad now, they can find a solution here. It's about work ethic [*sera behari*]. Some people might go and not have the right work ethic and end up jobless abroad too. Still, because they went and have seen other places and take things back, especially those who have been to Europe or America feel a bit better than people who have stayed here. The people coming from abroad have money and their perspectives have changed. When they start working with people here they feel a bit above them. They look down on people here and see them as uneducated and bad workers. This attitude might lead them to fail because they don't work hard themselves. Especially people with little education have difficulties doing business here after they return from abroad. Many lose all their money.

A few international migrants who returned could afford lifestyles that wealthy local businessmen struggled to match. Economic prospects were better abroad for some, but international migrants' limited education made my interlocutors question the social value of such strategies for increasing wealth. Uneducated international migrants who returned were envied for their economic capital, but their lack of higher education meant that their change in status was somewhat limited. Those without higher education who migrated abroad and made money circumvented the 'conventional' trajectory of increasing their wealth through higher education and employment, which sometimes frustrated people like Nebay who had studied at university, migrated internally and worked hard to prosper. His account of returnees' sense of superiority reveals his scepticism of the 'uneducated' regardless of their wealth. His analysis of why international returnees struggled to profit from their investments shows that he regarded uneducated people as less capable than those who were educated, reflecting how social distinctions were shaped because of the expansion of higher education.

In Ethiopia, some kinds of work are considered shameful (*yilunta*) and migration to other places in the country or abroad offers opportunities to take these kinds of work without the humiliation of family and friends knowing about it (Mains 2012). Although international migrants avoided the shame of 'bad' work by being elsewhere, many questioned how international migrants' who returned wealthy had earned their money abroad and their status remained ambiguous. There was also a gendered dimension to the shame of migration-related work as female migrants could be suspected of engaging in sex work or illicit sexual relations, especially those who were live-in domestic workers. These suspicions constituted a challenge to women's respectability, which wealth would not necessarily resolve. Such differences reflected existing gender roles, both in terms of how they responded to new opportunities and their aspirations for the future, as well as how the outcomes of their progress were received by others (which is the case in many countries, see e.g. Oduro and Nabalamba 2014).

Higher education degrees and subsequent employment enhanced one's material, symbolic and social capital. However, the prestige of higher education varied between different locations in Ethiopia. University education conferred higher status in rural areas and smaller towns where there were fewer people with such degrees than in bigger cities, as Medhane experienced when he migrated from Tigray to Addis Ababa. While the value of higher education degrees varied, the distinction between those who were educated and those who were not was often central to how my interlocutors perceived people's individual changes and status in relation to migration. The high cost of living in Addis Ababa made it impossible for Medhane and Elias to pursue the high lifestyles they had formerly associated with employment after higher education, but the highly visible inequalities in the capital also made them more aware that there were many people who struggled more than they did, which influenced how they thought about their own situation. One's education-related status varied and informed social relations differently depending on location, but urban-to-urban migration was still perceived as a means to progress.

The Social Value of Higher Education

The outcomes of higher education are often considered in relation to employment and income levels, but another aspect is individual status. Some have argued that higher education systems primarily serve to reproduce the privilege of elites and continue to limit prospects for students from other social backgrounds, even when they experience some changes in their lives because of their education (Bourdieu and Passeron 1990; Reay 2017). Similar accounts emerge from different places in Africa where higher education degrees, in some contexts, make unemployment preferable to 'low-skilled' jobs to avoid a decline in status (Masquelier 2013). Studies of international student migration have provided further nuance to the question of the relationship between higher education and social mobility by showing that the outcomes of higher education vary depending on differences between and within groups of international students that are exacerbated by, among other factors, length of study abroad (Waters and Leung 2013). Considering the many factors impacting on the outcomes of higher education, there is not a fixed relationship between higher education degrees obtained abroad and how they shape individuals' livelihoods (Collins et al. 2017). This applies also to migration for higher education within countries.

For my interlocutors in Ethiopia, the combination of internal migration and higher education shaped their distinct status. The majority of those who had studied and completed their higher education degrees had experienced an increase in wealth. Being educated conferred a certain status and opened new opportunities for employment, which meant that they could live with a higher degree of material comfort and be at the giving rather than the receiving end. For men, specifically, these shifts in circumstances enabled them to perform their masculinities as part of a gendered discourse around aspirations for prosperous urban lives. For many, this led to continued urban-to-urban migration to obtain employment that was more profitable or, even better, to establish their own businesses. In Tesfay's case, his higher education degree facilitated his migration between several cities for training and employment before he was finally able to start his own law firm and settle down in Addis Ababa.

Increased economic capital enabled my interlocutors to live and work in places where they could seek to adapt 'high lifestyles,' which many considered key to living a more fulfilling life. They often experienced shifts in their status in the years following the completion of their higher education degrees, as we saw with Aman who represented his university at a high-profile national event. These transformations in their lives demonstrate that the expansion of higher education and the introduction of cost-sharing widened opportunities for people from poor backgrounds. The degrees in themselves were important in facilitating broader employment choices, but people were also proactive in taking advantage of the possibilities that opened and pursue further progress. In Ortner's (2003) terms, they used their agency to negotiate class positioning, for example by spending part of their earnings to shift from being at the receiving end in reciprocal relationships to treating friends and acquaintances to drinks and meals. These performances, of converting economic capital into symbolic capital in public spaces, transformed their status and helped them establish new social relations. Conspicuous consumption and sharing with other people in similar socio-economic situations often led to new encounters and expanded social networks, which could lead to new jobs and business connections.

There have been several attempts to understand how the intersection of global images of what constitutes desirable lives and local notions of respectability shape middle-class practices (Lentz 2020). My interlocutors experienced changes in their daily lives, developed new tastes and consumption patterns through migration for higher education and subsequent employment, but this did not necessarily translate into upwards social mobility in a place like Addis Ababa. For Elias, and many others, the difference in the value of the same income between smaller cities and the capital was an obstacle to living the high life he had expected as a doctor. Even so, his migration and life in the capital influenced how he was perceived by others, but these perceptions differed between people in Adigrat and Addis Ababa, which complicates the idea of social mobility as a linear upward trajectory. Although individuals experienced enhanced material and symbolic capital, the value of these was not the same across locations. As a result, different class relations were produced simultaneously in the different locations where people had social relations.

This chapter has explored the social value of higher education that led to changes that could enhance people's status. The combination of my interlocutors' relative wealth with new practices shifted their positions in social relations. These processes point to yet another aspect of how their conceptualisations of progress and urban-to-urban migration made them different from those who did not engage in such migration, and illustrates that class positions are not simply reproduced (Spronk 2018). Instead, migration between cities contributed to creating a group whose commonalities were also what distinguished its members from others—their possession and use of forms of capital. These distinctions highlight that the formation of this middle class in Ethiopia is not only economic, but also relational, social and cultural. As the narratives in this chapter show, higher education is important in the creation of social hierarchies but, as Spronk (2020) suggests from Ghana, despite the importance of education in becoming middle class, on its own, it is not enough to achieve this status. The next chapter considers class formation further through a focus on how people managed shifting expectations and the competing meanings of progress that emerged from their urban-to-urban migration.

References

Adepoju, Aderanti. 2000. "Issues and Recent Trends in International Migration in Sub-Saharan Africa." *International Social Science Journal* 52 (165): 383–94. https://doi.org/10.1111/1468-2451.00267.

Admassu, Kassahun A. 2011. "Primary School Enrollment and Dropout in Ethiopia: Household and School Factors." In *Proceedings from Population Association of America 2011 Annual Meeting*, 1–42. Washington DC, USA: Princeton.

Akalu, Girmaw Abebe. 2014. "Higher Education in Ethiopia: Expansion, Quality Assurance and Institutional Autonomy." *Higher Education Quarterly* 68 (4): 394–415.

Apple, Michael, ed. 1982. *Cultural and Economic Reproduction in Education: Essays on Class, Ideology and the State*. London and Boston: Routledge and Kegan Paul Books.

Ashcroft, Kate, and Philip Rayner. 2012. "The Purposes and Practices of Quality Assurance in Ethiopian Higher Education: Journey, Adaptation and Integration." *International Journal of Business Anthropology* 3 (2): 19–25.

Ayalew, Sewale Abate. 2012. "Financing Higher Education in Ethiopia: Analysis of Cost-Sharing Policy and Its Implementation." *Higher Education Policy* 26 (1): 109–126 (Retraction published 11 June 2013).

Balsvik, Randi R. 2005. *The Quest for Expression: The University and State in Ethiopia Under Three Regimes, 1952–2003*. Wiesbaden: Harrassowitz Verlag.

Bourdieu, Pierre. 1984. *Distinction: A Social Critique of the Judgment of Taste*. Translated by R. Nice. Cambridge, MA: Harvard University Press.

———. 1986. "The Forms of Capital." In *Handbook of Theory and Research for the Sociology of Education*, edited by John G. Richardson, 241–258. New York: Greenwood Press.

Bourdieu, Pierre, and Jean-Claude Passeron. 1990. *Reproduction in Education, Society and Culture*. vol. 4. Sage.

Chaudhury, Nazmul, Mohammad Niaz Asadullah, and Luc Christiaensen. 2006. "Schools, Household, Risk, and Gender: Determinants of Child Schooling in Ethiopia." Working Paper CSAE WPS/2006-06. ESRC Centre on SKOPE, Oxford University.

Collins, Francis, Kong Chong Ho, Mayumi Ishikawa, and Ai-Hsuan Sandra Ma. 2017. "International Student Mobility and After-Study Lives: The Portability and Prospects of Overseas Education in Asia: International Student Mobility and After-Study Lives." *Population, Space and Place* 23 (4): e2029. https://doi.org/10.1002/psp.2029.

Cornwall, Andrea. 2005. "Introduction: Perspectives on Gender in Africa." In *Readings in Gender in Africa*, edited by Andrea Cornwall, 1–19. London: The International African Institute.

Delamont, Sara. 1989. *Knowledgeable Women: Structuralism and the Reproduction of Elites*. London and New York: Routledge.

Di Nunzio, Marco. 2019. *The Act of Living: Street Life, Marginality, and Development in Urban Ethiopia*. Cornell University Press.

Donham, Donald L. 1992. "Revolution and Modernity in Maale: Ethiopia, 1974 to 1987." *Comparative Studies in Society and History* 34 (1): 28–57.

Durham, Deborah. 2020. "Morality in the Middle: Choosing Cars or Houses in Botswana." *Africa* 90 (3): 489–508. https://doi.org/10.1017/S0001972020000042.

Ferguson, James. 1999. *Expectations of Modernity: Myths and Meanings of Urban Life on the Zambian Copperbelt*. Berkeley: University of California Press.

Heinonen, Paula. 2013. *Youth Gangs and Street Children: Culture, Nurture and Masculinity in Ethiopia*. New York: Berghahn Books.

King, Russell, and Parvati Raghuram. 2013. "International Student Migration: Mapping the Field and New Research Agendas." *Population, Space and Place* 19 (2): 127–37.

Krishnan, Pramila. 1996. "Family Background, Education and Employment in Urban Ethiopia." *Oxford Bulletin of Economics and Statistics* 58 (1): 167–83.

Kritz, Mary M. 2015. "International Student Mobility and Tertiary Education Capacity in Africa." *International Migration* 53 (1): 29–49. https://doi.org/10.1111/imig.12053.

Kroeker, Lena, David O'Kane, and Tabea Scharrer, eds. 2018. *Middle Classes in Africa: Changing Lives and Conceptual Challenges*. Frontiers of Globalization. Cham, Switzerland: Palgrave Macmillan. https://doi.org/10.1007/978-3-319-62148-7.

Lentz, Carola. 2016. "African Middle Classes: Lessons from Transnational Studies and a Research Agenda." *The Rise of Africa's Middle Class: Myths, Realties and Critical Engagements*, 17–53.

———. 2020. "Doing Being Middle-Class in the Global South: Comparative Perspectives and Conceptual Challenges." *Africa* 90 (3): 439–69. https://doi.org/10.1017/S0001972020000029.

Levine, Donald N. 1965. *Wax and Gold: Tradition and Innovation in Ethiopian Culture*. Chicago: University of Chicago Press.

Mains, Daniel. 2012. *Hope Is Cut: Youth, Unemployment, and the Future in Urban Ethiopia*. Philadelphia: Temple University Press.

Masquelier, A. 2013. "Teatime: Boredom and the Temporalities of Young Men in Niger." *Africa* 83 (3): 470–91.

Miescher, Stephan, and Lisa A Lindsay. 2003. "Introduction: Men and Masculinities in Modern African History." In *Men and Masculinities in Modern Africa*, edited by Lisa A Lindsay and Stephan Miescher, 1–29. Portsmouth, NH: Heinemann.

Milkias, Paulos. 2008. "Modernity, the Ethiopian Youth and the Challenge of the Third Millennium." *International Journal of Ethiopian Studies* 3 (2): 91–101.

Negewo-Oda, Beza, and Aaronette M. White. 2011. “Identity Transformation and Reintegration Among Ethiopian Women War Veterans: A Feminist Analysis.” *Journal of Feminist Family Therapy* 23 (3–4): 163–87. https://doi.org/10.1080/08952833.2011.604536.

Oduro and Nabalamba. 2014. “Gender.” In *The Emerging Middle Class in Africa*, edited by Mthuli Ncube and Charles Leyeka Lufumpa. Routledge.

Ogato, S. 2013. “The Quest for Gender Equality and Womens Empowerment in Least Developed Countries: Policy and Strategy Implications for Achieving Millennium Development Goals in Ethiopia.” *International Journal of Sociology and Anthropology* 5 (9): 358–72.

Ortner, Sherry B. 2003. *New Jersey Dreaming: Capital, Culture, and the Class of '58*. Duke University Press.

Ottaway, Marina. 1976. “Social Classes and Corporate Interests in the Ethiopian Revolution.” *The Journal of Modern African Studies* 14 (3): 469–86.

Pankhurst, Helen. 1992. *Gender, Development, and Identity: An Ethiopian Study*. London: Zed Books.

Poluha, Eva. 2007. “Research on Ethiopian Children: Subjects Covered and Possible New Themes.” In *The World of Girls and Boys in Rural and Urban Ethiopia*, edited by Eva Poluha, 181–211. Addis Ababa: Forum for Social Studies.

Reay, Diane. 2017. *Miseducation: Inequality, Education and the Working Classes*. Policy Press.

Riaño, Yvonne, Christof Van Mol, and Parvati Raghuram. 2018. “New Directions in Studying Policies of International Student Mobility and Migration.” *Globalisation, Societies and Education* 16 (3): 283–94. https://doi.org/10.1080/14767724.2018.1478721.

Semela, Tesfaye. 2011. “Breakneck Expansion and Quality Assurance in Ethiopian Higher Education: Ideological Rationales and Economic Impediments.” *Higher Education Policy* 24 (3): 399–425.

Spronk, Rachel. 2018. “Afterword. The (Idea of) African Middle Classes: Theorizing from Africa.” In *Middle Classes in Africa: Changing Lives and Conceptual Challenges*, edited by Lena Kroeker, David O'Kane, and Tabea Scharrer, 311–26. Cham, Switzerland: Palgrave Macmillan.

———. 2020. “Structures, Feelings and *Savoir Faire*: Ghana's Middle Classes in the Making.” *Africa* 90 (3): 470–88. https://doi.org/10.1017/S0001972020000030.

UNESCO. 2020. “Ethiopia.” 2020. http://uis.unesco.org/en/country/et.

Wagaw, Teshome G. 1990. *The Development of Higher Education and Social Change: An Ethiopian Experience*. East Lansing, Michigan: Michigan State University Press.

Waters, Johanna, and Rachel Brooks. 2011. "'Vive La Différence?': The 'International' Experiences of UK Students Overseas." *Population, Space and Place* 17 (5): 567–78. https://doi.org/10.1002/psp.613.

Waters, Johanna, and Maggi Leung. 2013. "Immobile Transnationalisms? Young People and Their in Situ Experiences of 'International' Education in Hong Kong." *Urban Studies* 50 (3): 606–20. https://doi.org/10.1177/0042098012468902.

Waweru, Kennedy M., Sewale Abate, Guyo H. Huka, and Shano M. Dawe. 2011. "Financing Higher Education in Africa: A Case of Ethiopia Public Universities Cost Containment Measures." *Educational Research* 2 (4): 1089–93.

Weiler, K. 1988. *Women Teaching for Change: Gender, Class & Power*. Westport, CN: Greenwood Publishing Group.

Willis, Paul E. 1977. *Learning to Labor: How Working Class Kids Get Working Class Jobs*. New York: Columbia University Press.

Woldehanna, Tassew, and Adiam Hagos. 2015. "Economic Shocks and Children's Dropout from Primary School: Implications for Education Policy in Ethiopia." *Africa Education Review* 12 (1): 28–47.

5

Managing Enhanced Capital

Distinctions within a Compound

In the preceding chapters, urban-to-urban migration in Ethiopia emerged as an important means for my interlocutors to progress. Here, I shift attention to how they attempted to navigate social relations amidst different and sometimes competing forms of progress. In Adigrat, I shared a room with Mehari in a walled compound generally occupied by 20–25 people. Staying there, I gained access to a number of people, including relatives passing through for shorter or longer stays, and could interact relatively freely with the female residents. Apart from Mehari's family, there were several other families renting single-room stone houses from his parents. These neighbours and tenants were poorer, had less education, worked in low-paid or informal jobs, and had different migration patterns than Mehari's family.

In one house, there was a woman in her forties from the nearby town of Wukro. She had married a man from Adigrat but had divorced him and now lived on her own, making a living by brewing and selling beer from her house. Next to my and Mehari's room, there was a woman from

M. R. Breines, *Becoming Middle Class*,
Globalization, Urbanization and Development in Africa,
https://doi.org/10.1007/978-981-16-3537-3_5

Eritrea who provided for her three teenage boys by growing vegetables which she sold in the market. In another one-room house, there was a married couple with three children: two teenage girls and a young boy of about a year. The woman, who was from Oromiaregion, stayed at home and her husband, a local, patrolled the streets at night for the militia and did odd jobs a few days a week. Another woman lived alone with her daughter. Her husband had left for Saudi Arabia to work as soon as their daughter had completed school and was old enough to manage the small clothes stall he had run in a street market for several years. These residents of the compound were not my main focus, but by observing and participating in the interactions between people in different social positions living next to each other I gradually developed an understanding of how they were distinct from Mehari and my other interlocutors who had higher education degrees and formal employment (Image 5.1).

Staying in this compound provided me with ample opportunities to observe how small and big occurrences in the compound were shaped

Image 5.1 Rental accommodation—a room for five people, Adigrat

by hierarchical relations. When Mehari's mother became paralysed after suffering a stroke prior to the start of my fieldwork, they had, as was common for families that could afford it, brought in a young female relative from the countryside to help out with daily chores in exchange for some financial support. On one occasion Rahel, Mehari's elder sister, told the domestic worker, Haben, to make butter. Normally the process should take about an hour, but it was only when Mehari walked by after three hours that he found out what was going on and made her stop. Rahel had insisted that Haben continue churning until it became butter and Mehari was angry with his sister saying; 'she's treating her like a slave.' Later, I asked Rahel what had happened and she told me that Haben was a *fara* (country bumpkin) who did not know how to do anything because of her rural origin. She illustrated her point with another example of when the Haben had been sent to buy a Mirinda from a nearby shop but had come back with Coca-Cola instead. Rahel's description of Haben's shortcomings can be seen in relation to ideas of the city as more developed and where people are more skilful and knowledgeable than those from backward rural areas who have limited understanding of city life (even if this did not explain Haben's inability to make butter). The practice of poorer relatives working for wealthier households is common in many parts of the world. This creates multi-class households (Lentz 2020) and points to the individual and family dimensions of middle-class formation (Hareven 1977). By spending time with people who lived in the compound, I gained insights into how people in different social positions conceptualised progress—Mehari's aspirations and prospects were very different from Haben's—and how these ideas were entrenched in social hierarchies.

In addition to differences between individuals and families, socio-economic changes in Africa have impacted people's capacity for progressing as expected. A case in point from Zambia is the privatisation of the housing market, which impeded young men's access to affordable accommodation in Lusaka which in turn impeded their opportunities to get married and set up a household (Hansen 2005). Instead, they ended up living with their parents for longer than expected which meant that they did not achieve adulthood at the appropriate age (ibid.). Many young people in Ethiopia face similar challenges in fulfilling their envisioned life trajectories. The EPRDF government's authoritarian approach to development and the implementation of neoliberal reforms since 1991 has influenced people's conceptualisations of progress. Ideas that 'everyone can do as he wants [sic]' have been central to how people have contested categories and given new meanings to hierarchical relations, for example by marrying across group boundaries, using new idioms and information and taking up new professions (Ellison 2006). Such changes have also made it clearer that there is not necessarily a relationship between national development and individual progress. Many of Mains' interlocutors considered Ethiopia to be developing because roads were being upgraded and multi-storeyed buildings constructed. The expectation was that these improvements would enhance employment, transport and business opportunities for local people—though many struggled to afford three meals a day and lived with unreliable water or power supply (Mains 2012a). As they are both processes, development and progress do not always intersect in ways that enable people to improve their lives.

People's responses to global economic trends and limited job openings vary, and notions of development and progress have commonly been explored in relation to how people in various African urban settings cope with decline (Mains 2012b; Masquelier 2013). In urban Senegal, young men were disparaged for not prospering even though their unemployment and marginalisation was an outcome of postcolonial economic stagnation, but they found an alternative in preparing and serving tea, which offered them an opportunity to engage in a meaningful practice that helped them avoid becoming 'pathologically unproductive subject[s]' (Ralph 2008). Interestingly, tea brewing also became a meaningful activity among young men struggling to find employment, purpose and direction in Niger (Masquelier 2013). Neither in Senegal nor in Niger did this practice generate any major material progress, but this alternative activity enabled the young men to maintain a degree of status despite declining economic prospects and lack of employment. Somewhat similarly, in the Ivory Coast, unemployed men, known as *les bluffeurs* (bluffers), drew upon local ideas of modernity to trick people and obtain money, material goods and status (Newell 2012). *Les bluffeurs*' proactive use of modernity as both a discourse and a social skill to make a living for themselves under conditions of unemployment and economic hardship diverges from perspectives suggesting that modernity is a condition that cannot be achieved (e.g. Latour 1993), and shows how it becomes a 'reality' that can be used to contest social hierarchies. This chapter focuses on people who were 'productive' in economic terms, but, like the bluffers, my interlocutors' distinct meanings of progress shaped their life trajectories. Still, their diverse social relations impacted on how they experienced the outcomes of their progress.

Metamorphosing Wealth into Status

My interlocutors would not emigrate abroad for wealth, but many of them aspired to become richer within Ethiopia. Such aspirations were often expressed in relation to their interest in supporting others, as Haftay implied: 'I'm planning to become rich to help my family. You'll be happy if you're rich.' There is a clear relationship between wealth and status, but the status implications of wealth are also influenced by how people use or distribute their money. Rather than relying on others' generosity, being able to provide for family and friends and contribute to their well-being, would enable one to live a more satisfactory life, with fewer worries (*chnq*).

The richest man in Ethiopia, Mohammed Hussein Al Amoudi, was regularly mentioned in everyday conversations. Ranked the 138th richest person in the world (Forbes 2016), he was well-known to many Ethiopians. His great wealth was primarily talked about in terms of his contributions to the development of the country by establishing numerous factories and giving Ethiopians employment. This was pointed out by one of my fellow travellers on the Selam Bus who told me as we passed through the town of Kombolcha: 'All the factories here are set up by Al Amoudi, he has turned Kombolcha into an industrial zone.' Many admired him for his wealth and what he had done for Ethiopia, and regularly referred to his generosity and reputation for social engagement and helping the poor.

Another time Al Amoudi became the centre of conversation was after doctors in Addis Ababa had informed Tesfay that they could not perform surgery on his heart. His condition was too serious for them to operate on him and the doctors suggested that his best option was to go to Thailand for surgery. The price for such an operation would come to about $17,000, a very large sum for my interlocutors. Friends of Tesfay in different cities began collecting money, and Mehari also composed a text message which he sent out to everybody in his vast contact list. He walked through Adigrat, stopping in shops and restaurants and approaching friends and acquaintances on the street. Initially, many people donated 100 birr [$5.40], but after a few days the amounts decreased, and he was becoming frustrated by the lack of progress. Some people even gave as little as 10 birr [$0.54]. Soon, Mehari realised that Tesfay might not survive the time it would take to collect the amount needed for the operation:

> *Mehari*: The problem would be solved if I could get hold of Al Amoudi.
> *Markus*: Why?
> *Mehari*: He always helps people who are too ill to be treated in Ethiopia. For example, some years back there was a case where a woman was attacked by her partner with acid [which was not common in Ethiopia], and Al Amoudi covered the woman's face-restoring operations in Europe. He would definitively donate money to help Tesfay out. The problem is how to reach him.

It was often through generosity that wealth became valuable in social relations and central to individuals' status. Al Amoudi was respected for his enormous wealth, but his perceived generosity was also central to his status. My interlocutors were in very different economic situations to Al Amoudi, but they also shaped their social relations through generosity and sharing their wealth with family, friends, and acquaintances.

As a researcher, I was entangled in financial dynamics of social relationships during (and after) the fieldwork. I stood out because of my appearance, and there was also an assumption that my skin colour and European nationality meant that I was wealthy. These assumptions are in many cases correct as foreigners from Europe and North America are often wealthier than many Ethiopians, but the cost of Tesfay's surgery was well beyond what I could afford. My inability to save his life with a large donation was frustrating, but it also raised ethical questions about my role as a researcher. There were many others who needed support and making decisions about who to help were often difficult. It is well established that anthropologists do not pay their research participants for information, but the social relations that are established during long-term research often make it impossible to exclude money. Like my interlocutors who shared their wealth with less fortunate people, I also shared in situations where it was appropriate, such as buying dinners for people and giving donations to people in need (often following Mehari's and others' lead as I did not have the cultural capital to understand what would be appropriate in each situation). Many people also paid for my drinks and meals against my will or without my knowledge. These gestures and the social play around them strengthened the ties between us. Nevertheless, the case of Tesfay was particularly challenging to me and in the end, I donated the same amount as Mehari (waiting to see if I could potentially provide a larger donation if they were getting anywhere close to the required amount). In the end, a religious organisation in Wukro donated the money he needed, and, eventually, he moved to Addis Ababa to establish a law practice (Chapter 3).

More commonly, my interlocutors shared their material wealth in everyday life. Mehari's youngest sister, Kidisti, was studying at Bahir Dar University and regularly phoned him for financial support, either for daily expenses or when she needed money for medical treatment and travel. One morning, Mehari's phone started ringing while we were still asleep. After he had spoken to Kidisti, I asked Mehari why she kept calling him and not someone else for money. He responded: 'People always ask me because I'm easy-going compared to my brother and father. They will ask what they will do with the money and question if they really need it. If I have money, I will give it.' A few hours later, we walked to the bank to wire 500 birr [$27] to her. There were lots of people lined up at the different counters in the bank and as we were waiting for Mehari's turn a young man came walking in between two policemen. Mehari pulled some money out of his pocket and went over to him to give him 50 birr [$2.70], which the man gratefully accepted. After Mehari had sent the money to Kidisti and we were out on the street again, I asked Mehari who the man was.

Mehari: I have seen him around before, but I don't know him. I know he's got a long sentence and has already been in prison for several years.
Markus: So why did you give him money?
Mehari: It's normal to support and give money to people who have problems. It's like insurance. If I give to those who are struggling now, people will help me when I need it. It's the same for visiting sick people and going to weddings and funerals. I have to go so that people will come for me later.

There was a degree of self-interest in being generous as sharing of wealth converted people's economic capital into symbolic capital (Bourdieu 1986). Mehari's emphasis on material support for people in need and social support for events such as weddings and funerals illustrate that generosity also had a non-material side. People from all backgrounds could fulfil social expectations of non-material generosity by attending weddings, baptisms and mourning ceremonies, but those who were able to combine material and non-material generosity obtained a different status. In other words, Mehari's sharing practices reflected his possession of capital, through which he negotiated social relations and his position within them.

People's strong sense of obligation to support their families and to share more widely gave impetus to my interlocutors' aspirations to become richer. Gidey, a man in his early thirties who had grown up in poverty had, together with some of his siblings, set up a hotel, a bar, a shop and a restaurant, and had plans for further expansion:

Gidey: I'm considering other options now, maybe buying a truck to empty septic tanks.
Markus: You have so many businesses already, are you trying to become rich like Al Amoudi?
Gidey: Yes, I've got fifteen siblings, I need a lot of money to support all of them.

Some referred to becoming rich as essential for them to fulfil strongly felt social obligations to kin. Sharing their wealth was common among men and these practices resonated with their ideas of being able to provide for their families. Sharing with non-kin was not obligatory in the same sense, but such relationships also had a material dimension. Mains (2013, 344) shows that friendships in urban Ethiopia depend on balancing affection and reciprocity, and that rather than being a means to an end, the 'relationship between material wealth and affection is mutually constitutive.' My interlocutors' aspirations for increased wealth and their practices of sharing with others show how economic capital is made socially meaningful in this context. Through fulfilling social expectations of sharing both with kin and non-kin they would increase their status. Wealth influenced individuals' social positions, but their status also depended on the amounts and frequency of their sharing practices.

Both Mehari and Gidey made enough money in Adigrat to be able to share some of their material wealth, but for many others, migration was perceived to be central for finding the kinds of jobs that could make them richer. But, despite the potential for prosperity and progress, migration to other cities could also potentially influence their behaviour and make their engagement in social relations less 'traditional' (*bahelawi*). In smaller towns and rural areas, relations to family and people were said to take priority over individuals' needs and desires, as Mehari explained:

> In the countryside, people respect other people and guests. They are very kind. In Addis Ababa, if guests are coming, people switch off their phones so they don't have to host and take care of them. They think only about getting more for themselves, not about other people.

There was an understanding that people who migrated to bigger cities could change from being generous towards becoming more self-centred. My interlocutors spoke of the shifting priorities of people as a direct outcome of living in more modern places. Senait, an NGO worker (see Chapter 2), said:

> It is said that people from Addis Ababa don't like their relatives. I have heard that they are becoming like Europeans. For example, in Adigrat you don't have to ask to visit your family, you can just go there and stay there for a week or two. In Addis Ababa, you have to ask them in advance if you want to stay for two or three days.

In the capital, social interaction and strong social relations were thought to have been replaced with more modern (*zemenawi*) attitudes that placed the individual above social responsibilities. Through migration to Addis Ababa, people could become more knowledgeable about the world and its diversity, but this also carried the risk of making them more individualistic and less inclined to care for others. Such behaviours were considered to be in stark contrast to the more social ways of living that interlocutors portrayed as their culture (*bahel*) in Tigray, and the narratives of these differences required them to find strategies to manage social relationships both in relation to the realities of living in the capital and expectations of maintaining their connections with their cultural origin (Image 5.2). Vaughan (2012) argues that the experience of rapid societal transformation and modernity cannot sufficiently meet people's emotional needs, and, in this case, migration to bigger cities generates tensions between different sets of values. These discrepancies suggest that migration did not unequivocally lead to the enhancement of status. The potential for metamorphosing wealth into status depended upon how people manoeuvred social relations in new places while fulfilling social expectations and moral obligations that corresponded to a different set

Image 5.2 Early evening street scene, Addis Ababa

of values. This way of coping with different expectations suggests that changes in individuals' possession and use of capital through migration produced tensions between their shifting status and social obligations.

Urban-to-urban migration posed challenges for people to maintain traditional (*bahelawi*) forms of social relations, but also helped them overcome the perceived backwardness of Adigrat and enhanced their symbolic capital as they became seen as city people. For them, it was possible to increase their economic capital through internal migration to bigger cities rather than international migration, but these movements also contributed to shift social relations. Responsibilities towards family and relatives were often felt less intensely with physical distance, though, back home, expectations of migrants' capacity to share often increased. These tensions between individualism and social obligations (see also Mercer and Lemanski 2020) led some of my interlocutors to avoid returning to their place of origin for extended periods. Their shifting attitudes to what they considered to be traditional family relations and obligations do not necessarily imply the formation of greater individualism, but that increasing expectations sometimes exceeded people's material progress. The social distinctions and hierarchical relations that were formed through migration were partly outcomes of their growing skill in manoeuvring tensions between competing forms of progress.

Competing Forms of Progress

It was a common aspiration among my interlocutors to go to Addis Ababa, which was often spoken about as the most attractive city in Ethiopia. Migration to bigger cities with access and diversity could turn them into city people, which constituted a form of progress to them, but there were also other aspects of life that could impede their progress in bigger cities. The cost of living in capital cities is often higher than elsewhere, and Addis Ababa is no exception.

In many cases, standards of living were lowered when they settled down in Addis Ababa. The economic realities in Addis Ababa were different from the rest of the country and a few years before Tesfay moved to the capital, he pointed out: 'If I get a job with the same salary as I'm getting now I'll be very poor in Addis Ababa. The cost of living is very high. If I had enough money I would have been in Addis Ababa already.' This was a common concern for those who considered migrating to the capital. Those who had made the move to Addis Ababa and worked in the public sector faced the kind of challenges that Tesfay mentioned. During a visit to the capital, Senait, who lived in Mekelle at the time, observed:

> Life is difficult for people in Addis Ababa. For example, I have seen my sister's life. She's a public prosecutor and her salary, 2,500 birr [$135] a month, is not different from what people in the same position get in other regions. Because of the expensive housing she lives far away from where she works, and she has to get up at 5am to get ready to leave. She can't take lunch for her son at the day-care and she gets home late at night. To me this seems like a difficult life.

The long distances and difficulty of travelling on slow and overcrowded public transport made it harder for people to maintain strong social relations as they had done in Adigrat. The high cost of living also made it impossible for many to live up to the expectations that followed from their urban lifestyles. My interlocutors were, to some extent, aware of conditions in the capital, but many migrated there or aspired to do so in the future regardless. Why would they want to live in a place where their social and economic quality of life might be reduced?

Access and diversity were key factors in shaping their intentions to migrate to Addis Ababa. In order to migrate and overcome the economic challenges in the capital, some tried to position themselves to get better jobs there prior to migration. Samuel had bachelor's and master's degrees and was a lecturer at Mekelle University with a monthly salary of 3,300 birr [$178.20]. In the evenings, he studied for a bachelor's degree in economics. I was surprised that he had gone back to university, but he pointed out that it was part of his migration plan: 'I would be happy to live in Addis Ababa, but you have to have money to survive there. A normal income is not enough and the only way I can live there is if I get a job with an international NGO. That's why I'm studying economics.' It was primarily through private-sector employment or by having their own businesses that my interlocutors considered it possible to immerse themselves fully in the wide possibilities of upmarket lifestyles in Addis Ababa. Several pursued second or third higher education degrees to widen their opportunities to get the kinds of highly paid jobs that would enable them to live fulfilling lives in the capital. Rather than increasing wealth for its own sake, it was the capacity to lead other lifestyles that meant progress to Samuel and others.

Urban-to-urban migration was a common strategy for making the transition into better employment. Medhane, who had worked as a teacher for several years until he moved to the capital to find employment in the private sector as a construction site manager (see Chapter 4), said:

> There is a lot of hope for me in Addis Ababa now and I have two opportunities to progress here. I can develop my career at the construction site by doing building plans, and the other option is to get another job as an engineer after I finish my degree [through evening classes]. In Adigrat, you don't progress because you don't have to think and you only guess your expenses. You can live for 1,000 birr [$54] a month, and it will cover house rent, food and everything, but you will live like that for 30–40 years. If you like, you drink juice. Here it's not like that, you have to work all the time and think a lot. You have to budget all the expenses to survive, plan how much you have to use for transport, food and so on. Everything is expensive here. Even a 1x1 metre room where you have to leave the door open to lie down is expensive. In Addis Ababa, you will go through hardship for some time, that's mandatory, but then you will leave behind the problems.

While employment in a place like Adigrat offered a relatively comfortable life, this convenience was spoken about as a condition that contributed to people's backwardness (*hwalaqernet*). Working in Adigrat was not associated with prospects for prosperity, and the lack of opportunities for progress would lead people who stayed to settle for an easy life with little improvement in their lives. By migrating to Addis Ababa, my interlocutors anticipated progress in terms of becoming more knowledgeable about the world and obtaining employment that, over time, would enable them to live more fulfilling lives and increase their economic capital.

The very different circumstances in Addis Ababa were not only an issue for migrants, but also impacted how I conducted research there. In the capital, I often stayed in a cheap hotel in the Piazza neighbourhood, which did not afford me the same intimate knowledge of people's lives as in Adigrat where I shared a room with Mehari and lived next to his family, relatives and other residents in the compound. To meet and socialise with people who had higher education and were employed in formal jobs in Addis Ababa, I was reliant on making appointments in advance. This meant that I often spent time with my interlocutors in cafes, restaurants and bars in specific neighbourhoods and at times of the day when they were available. I also visited people in their homes in apartment buildings and villas in different parts of the city. Upon such visits, I was often invited for meals or coffee and introduced to relatives and neighbours, making these informal events opportunities to conduct participant observation of social life in private spaces. Drinking coffee prepared in the 'traditional' way allowed me to take part in spaces where people discussed their everyday lives, problems and supported each other (Yedes et al. 2004). These visits and interactions gave me insights into living conditions and made it clear to me that these circumstances were different from how people socialised in Adigrat.

Walking with people was another method I used. These walks through various neighbourhoods of Addis Ababa made it possible for me to gain new perspectives on their knowledge and understanding of the city. During walks, people told me about the buildings we passed, the churches we saw and sometimes entered, what the predominant ethnic group in certain areas were, the names and origin of rich people who owned hotels and businesses, and introduced me to friends and acquaintances we met by chance on the streets. Through such observations, I deepened my relationships with interlocutors and enhanced my understanding of how people experienced and 'saw' the city. In the words of Kusenbach (2003, 478), walking as method makes 'visible and intelligible how everyday experience transcends the here and now, as people weave previous knowledge and biography into immediate situated action.' This did not, however, fully compensate for the lack of continuous participant observation I was able to conduct during the lengthy periods of time I spent with people in Adigrat.

The limitations to conducting fieldwork in Addis Ababa helped me develop an understanding of the social conditions many migrants faced in the capital. To compensate, I immersed myself into the social life of mobile phone communication. Cheap phone calls have enabled people to maintain their social relations across large distances (Vertovec 2004), and mobile phone subscriptions in Ethiopia increased from 17,575 in 2000 to about 40 million in 2017 (ITU 2020). This expansion in mobile phone usage impacted on people's communication practices domestically and internationally, and these changes have also influenced how anthropologists interact with research participants (Hannerz 1998; Pelckmans 2009). When I was in Addis Ababa, I often called and received calls from friends in Adigrat as well as with people in other parts of the capital. The conversations were sometimes brief chats with people just to stay in touch and at other times of a more practical nature to make travel arrangements or set up meetings. By participating in a form of social life that was less bound to physical location, I gained insight into the forms of communication people practiced when separated by migration and physical distance.

The difficulties of socialising provided me with insights into migrants' social realities and were reflected in my more limited participant observation in the capital. The forms of social interactions in Addis Ababa were a recurrent issue in conversations with people, as were cost of living, employment, ethnic relations, distances and transport challenges. Such differences, and the new social relations and different behavioural codes (see also Ndlovu 2020) they navigated in the capital, made my interlocutors different from those who remained in Adigrat.

Public Versus Private Employment

Another factor that distinguished my interlocutors from people in other socio-economic positions was their intention and capacity to work in the private sector or establish their own businesses. This was a common trajectory; out of the 36 people I interviewed, 13 worked in the private sector and eight had their own businesses. The remaining 15 were either students looking for employment or were working in the public sector. Even so, like the other 21 interviewees, they considered working in the private sector or establishing their own businesses to be more attractive options. Mehari's youngest sister, Lemlem, had been staying with and looking after their mother while she was recovering from a stroke, but when I asked her what kind of work she aspired to have in the future, she said: 'I want to have my own business, not to work for the government (*yemengist sera*).' Such aspirations were often framed in relation to economic opportunities, though becoming richer was, as shown above, primarily framed in terms of being able to support family, relatives, friends and others.

Seeking private-sector employment and establishing their own businesses was common among my interlocutors. One day Nebay, who had his own accounting and financial service company, stopped by Adigrat in between his frequent travels in the region; he showed me a video on his smartphone of the desolate landscape outside Humera, close to the border to Sudan, where he had set up a stone crushing company. He explained the logic behind his effort to establish yet another business: 'The salary was enough to get by on when I did government work and it was secure because the job was permanent, but I make more money now. If one does private work (*yegil sera*) one can build a house and buy other things.' Nebay's trajectory, from a secure job with a fixed salary to private-sector employment and subsequently to establish his own businesses, had made him wealthier. By enhancing economic capital within Ethiopia, he and others maintained less ambiguous social status than international migrants who did bad or lower work to prosper, and were therefore also in better positions to convert their economic capital into symbolic capital.

In contrast to Nebay, who focused his businesses on smaller cities and rural contexts, the majority of my interlocutors considered there to be more opportunities for private-sector employment and setting up businesses in places with better 'access' (see Chapter 2) and diversity, such as Addis Ababa. Several people I spoke to in the capital had already moved on from the public sector. In 2015, while Tesfay and I were having dinner in the Hayahulett neighbourhood of Addis Ababa, two people he knew entered the restaurant and joined us at our table. Tesfay introduced me to Fitsum and Adhane, both in their forties, and as we ate Tesfay told me more about them:

Tesfay: They are both from Tigray but have lived in Addis Ababa for many years. I used to work with this fellow [grabbing Adhane's shoulder]. He was a judge, but now he has started his own company.
Markus: Really? Why did you quit?
Adhane: The salary was too low and there is no progress if you do government work.
Tesfay: Like everyone else he wants to become rich!

Despite the security and stable salary of his job, Adhane had opted to start his own advertising business instead. I had heard many narratives from people who made similar career changes, but I was a bit surprised that Adhane had given up such a high position which it would have taken him many years to obtain.

For those who still worked in the public sector, it was a common aspiration to eventually make this shift. Hewan had moved from Adigrat to Addis Ababa to study for a bachelor's degree in electrical and computer engineering and had subsequently found employment for a government agency. She was studying for a master's degree part-time on the weekends and in the evenings, and told me that she intended to move into the private sector after graduating: 'I'm planning to start my own work. Maybe after five years when I have more experience, I can set up my own company. I can hire people and make good progress for myself.' Shifting from public sector employment to the private sector or to establishing one's own business was often referred to as 'progress.' A central aspect of progress related to the opportunities it generated for increased economic capital, but, as discussed above, the importance of this was that it could be converted into symbolic capital. The tendency of highly educated people to leave jobs that were very attractive to less-educated people points to how education shaped employment trajectories, but also how these shifts shaped distinctions.

Some of my interlocutors wanted to work more directly for the benefit of society. Senait, who had worked for an NGO in Adigrat after completing her bachelor's degree and quit her job to pursue a master's degree in development studies in Mekelle, was eager to help people: 'There are many challenges for women in Ethiopia. I want to work on gender issues to improve the conditions for women in my country, for example for an NGO or some other job.' Such aspirations were not explicitly related to increasing economic capital, but rather to employing skills for the benefit of others. Tekle, a man from Tigray, told me: 'I'm a member of the EPRDF, but I want to advance and become a politician. For money it's better to be a businessman, but I want to serve the country and the people.' The diversity in people's aspirations for employment and their work trajectories yet again highlights that improvement in interlocutors' lives through employment was not only about higher salaries, but also related to their capacity to support people in less fortunate positions than themselves. Both Senait and Tekle aspired to obtain employment that would not necessarily give them much economic capital, but their social engagement would situate them so they would be respected, at least by some, for their dedication to develop Ethiopia. Nonetheless, such positions did generally pay relatively well and gave access to networks and power, which may have been an important motivation even if it was framed in other terms.

My interlocutors' meanings of progress were instrumental in their choices to engage in migration between urban centres, but different trajectories could constitute progress. This kind of migration appealed to them because it offered them both access and diversity, as well as prospects for increasing their wealth. Whereas becoming richer through international migration meant progress to people who struggled to get by in Ethiopia, to my interlocutors it depended upon pursuing particular forms of employment that would enable them to build symbolic capital. The conditions for increasing this form of capital in Addis Ababa were conflicting. There was access and diversity, but, at the same time, those who moved there faced, or could face, economic hardship and therefore also a lower quality of life. The high cost of living would reduce their capacity to share, which contrasted with their ideas of the relationship between progress and social relations. But the challenges in the capital were perceived as temporary obstacles that would be overcome over time.

The Challenges of Change

Conceptualisations of progress and the role of migration in managing diverse and sometimes conflicting expectations add another dimension to how my interlocutors became socially distinct from others. As shown in the preceding chapters, being in places associated with access and diversity gave them new experiences and widened their knowledge, but well-paid employment as a result of higher education enhanced their status further if they used and distributed their wealth in culturally appropriate ways. The general pattern of my interlocutors' transformations through urban-to-urban migration for higher education as well as employment, combined with their individual practices and skills in managing competing forms of progress, meant that the social outcomes of migration varied. Spronk (2020) warns that research participants easily end up presenting their experiences of upwards social mobility as lists of successes, but in my research, I found many experienced a range of difficulties that they often shared openly (at least with me). Their non-linear trajectories of improvement in their lives can be understood in relation to differences in the values of capital between locations, which made it difficult to construct a narrative of clear-cut progress.

Employment after higher education enabled my interlocutors to fulfil social relations through reciprocity (Mercer and Lemanski 2020), and thereby shift their positions within these relations. Even so, many of them aspired for more wealth than merely being able to sustain their livelihoods and treating others to drinks and meals. A wider distribution of their wealth was required to convert money into status. Mehari did this by sharing his accumulated wealth with his siblings and parents as well as friends and acquaintances. His capacity to support them financially distinguished him from those who supported others primarily in non-material terms. The possession and locally meaningful use of economic capital contributed to generating distinctions between those who could share and those who were not in positions to share as much.

Nonetheless, money could not buy status. Rather, it had to be combined with non-material generosity. This meant that values that centred around social relations could not be ignored in the pursuit of other forms of progress. The sometimes conflicting meanings of progress generated tensions in people's relationships with family and friends who expected them to be available and to share more because of their increasing status and therefore (assumed) wealth. Migration could also enable them to avoid some of their social responsibilities by maintaining a physical distance from their families and relatives, pointing to shifting expectations and strategies of responding to them. My interlocutors' pursuit of progress unfolded over several years and their meanings of progress changed to some extent as their social positions shifted. The challenges of upwards social mobility were also recognised by Bourdieu (1984) who found that such transformations could lead to a fragmented self because of the mismatch between people's different contextual social roles and positions. As such, the capacity to operate diverse sets of social relations amid increases in economic capital and status distinguished my interlocutors from people who possessed less capital, as well as those who were less skilled in responding to social expectations.

Conceptualisations of progress and the management of competing forms of progress add another dimension to the formation of the group of people I describe as being middle class in Ethiopia. Their meanings of progress reflect the shared cultural practices that emerge through migration, but also through their aspirations for specific forms of employment. Their preference for private-sector employment and desire to ultimately set up their own businesses contrasts to narratives of young Nigerien men's aspirations for public sector employment (Masquelier 2013). To my interlocutors, the stability and relatively low salaries of public sector employment did not offer the opportunity for continued progress, whereas migration to other urban centres opened the door to finding more attractive employment and enhancing their status in ways that corresponded with their conceptualisations of progress.

In this chapter, I have demonstrated that meanings of progress are related to different forms and values of capital. Economic capital was central because it could be converted into symbolic capital, if a balance between material and non-material sharing could be achieved. Progress, then, meant an increase of material and symbolic capital, but these increases needed to be guided by cultural capital to mean progress in environments where the tensions between different values became evident. Urban-to-urban migration contributed to enhance my interlocutors' possession of economic capital and facilitated its conversion into symbolic capital. Their cultural capital remained a factor that, to some extent, constrained their social mobility because its value differs between locations and cannot simply be modified to work in new contexts (Erel 2010). This is partly linked to class being relational, and the value of individual transformations depending on the continuous negotiations and assessments of each other's possession and use of capital. In the next chapter, I turn the focus to ethnicity to consider social capital and the relational aspects of class in more detail.

References

Bourdieu, Pierre. 1984. *Distinction: A Social Critique of the Judgment of Taste.* Translated by R. Nice. Cambridge, MA: Harvard University Press.

———. 1986. "The Forms of Capital." In *Handbook of Theory and Research for the Sociology of Education*, edited by John G. Richardson, 241–58. New York: Greenwood Press.

Ellison, James. 2006. "'Everyone Can Do as He Wants': Economic Liberalization and Emergent Forms of Antipathy in Southern Ethiopia." *American Ethnologist* 33 (4): 665–86.

Erel, Umut. 2010. "Migrating Cultural Capital: Bourdieu in Migration Studies." *Sociology* 44 (4): 642–60.

Forbes. 2016. "The World's Billionaires." The World's Billionaires. http://www.forbes.com/profile/mohammed-al-amoudi/#.

Hannerz, Ulf. 1998. "Transnational Research." In *Handbook of Methods in Cultural Anthropology*, edited by H.R. Bernard, 235–58. Walnut Creek, CA: AltaMira.

Hansen, Karen Tranberg. 2005. "Getting Stuck in the Compound: Some Odds Against Social Adulthood in Lusaka, Zambia." *Africa Today* 51 (4): 3–16.

Hareven, Tamara K. 1977. "Family Time and Historical Time." *Daedalus*, 57–70.

ITU. 2020. "Statistics." May 8. https://www.itu.int/en/ITU-D/Statistics/Pages/stat/default.aspx.

Kusenbach, Margarethe. 2003. "Street Phenomenology: The Go-Along as Ethnographic Research Tool." *Ethnography* 4 (3): 455–85.

Latour, Bruno. 1993. *We Have Never Been Modern*. Cambridge, MA: Harvard University Press.

Lentz, Carola. 2020. "Doing Being Middle-Class in the Global South: Comparative Perspectives and Conceptual Challenges." *Africa* 90 (3): 439–69. https://doi.org/10.1017/S0001972020000029.

Mains, Daniel. 2012a. "Blackouts and Progress: Privatization, Infrastructure, and a Developmentalist State in Jimma, Ethiopia." *Cultural Anthropology* 27 (1): 3–27.

———. 2012b. *Hope Is Cut: Youth, Unemployment, and the Future in Urban Ethiopia*. Philadelphia: Temple University Press.

———. 2013. "Friends and Money: Balancing Affection and Reciprocity Among Young Men in Urban Ethiopia." *American Ethnologist* 40 (2): 335–46. https://doi.org/10.1111/amet.12025.

Masquelier, Adeline. 2013. "Teatime: Boredom and the Temporalities of Young Men in Niger." *Africa* 83 (3): 470–91.

Mercer, Claire, and Charlotte Lemanski. 2020. "The Lived Experiences of the African Middle Classes Introduction." *Africa* 90 (3): 429–38. https://doi.org/10.1017/S0001972020000017.

Ndlovu, Thabisani. 2020. "Shuttling Between the Suburbs and the Township: The New Black Middle Class(es) Negotiating Class and Post-Apartheid Blackness in South Africa." *Africa* 90 (3): 568–86. https://doi.org/10.1017/S000197202000008X.

Newell, Sasha. 2012. *The Modernity Bluff: Crime, Consumption, and Citizenship in Côte D'Ivoire*. Chicago and London: University of California Press.

Pelckmans, L. 2009. "Phoning Anthropologists: The Mobile Phone's (Re-)shaping of Anthropological Research." In *Mobile Phones: The New Talking Drums of Everyday Africa*, edited by M. de Bruijn, Francis B. Nyamnjoh, and I. Brinkman, 23–49. Bamenda, Cameroon and Leiden, The Netherlands: Langaa & African Studies Centre.

Ralph, M. 2008. "Killing Time." *Social Text* 26 (4): 1–29.

Spronk, Rachel. 2020. "Structures, Feelings and *Savoir Faire* : Ghana's Middle Classes in the Making." *Africa* 90 (3): 470–88. https://doi.org/10.1017/S0001972020000030.

Vaughan, Mary Kay. 2012. "Labor Professionalization, Class Formation, and State Rule." In *The Making of the Middle Class: Toward a Transnational History*, edited by López and Weinstein. Durham NC: Duke University Press.

Vertovec, Steven. 2004. "Cheap Calls: The Social Glue of Migrant Transnationalism." *Global Networks* 4 (2): 219–24.
Yedes, Janet, Robbin Clamons, and Amal Osman. 2004. "Buna: Oromo Women Gathering for Coffee." *Journal of Contemporary Ethnography* 33 (6): 675–703.

6

Ethnic Hierarchies

Presuming and Contesting Ethnic Privilege

When I mentioned to people in Addis Ababa that I had been spending time in the Tigray region, several mentioned the Tigrayan political dominance under the EPRDF[1] and referred to Tigrayans as a distinct and privileged group. Habte, a man in his late twenties from Nazret who identified as Oromo and was working as a hairdresser in the capital, suggested that his predicament of low-paid employment and poor prospects for improving his livelihood was a result of the EPRDF government favouring Tigray:

Markus: How do you feel about Meles Zenawi [the former prime minister] passing away?

Habte: I'm happy, he had been in power too long. On TV, they showed only people crying, but in the streets people were cheering. Meles was a thief. He was just like Saddam and Gaddafi, killing any opposition.

[1] The lead party in the multi-ethnic EPDRF coalition was the Tigray People's Liberation Front, which was also the party of its long-term prime minister Meles Zenawi.

M. R. Breines, *Becoming Middle Class*,
Globalization, Urbanization and Development in Africa,
https://doi.org/10.1007/978-981-16-3537-3_6

Markus: Are you not exaggerating?
Habte: No, there is no work here and all the tax goes to Tigray.
Markus: How do you know that the government allocates more money to Tigray? Have you been there?
Habte: No, I haven't, but Tigrayans are always wearing gold rings and necklaces.

Many of my non-Tigrayan interlocutors in Addis Ababa considered the subjugation of the broader Ethiopian population a government strategy to deprive the rest of the country of power and resources in favour of the Tigray region. Tigrayans living outside Tigray were also considered to benefit from their ethnic affiliation with the EPRDF government in terms of financial advantages based on the extraction of resources from the rest of Ethiopia.

These perceptions of the benefits of being Tigrayan were not limited to people who lived precarious lives on small incomes. More affluent people shared the sense of state-imposed ethnic inequality. Hana, a fifty-year-old who was classified on her identification card as a 'foreign national of Ethiopian origin,' had been educated in Europe and lived there for more than two decades. She stated: 'It is said that a lot of resources are going to the north [Tigray], that nice hospitals and factories are being built there. I think Tigray is favoured because the government is controlled by Tigrayans.' This discontent with the distribution of resources to Tigray and the related deprivation in other parts of the country (see also Abbink 2017) reflects a broader narrative of ethnic inequality where Tigrayans were positioned at the top of the hierarchy.

The injustice of ethnic-based inequalities was regularly expressed through protests. In 2016, there were violent demonstrations against the EPRDF in the Amhara and Oromia regions and several people were killed. The government responded with a state of emergency that lasted for about ten months. This did not abate discontent with the regime and an ensuing power struggle within the EPRDF led to Abiy Ahmed becoming prime minister in 2018. His Oromo background and new leadership approach were welcomed and met with optimism among many Ethiopians. The normalisation of relations with Eritrea, release of political prisoners and return of exiled opposition leaders were important steps to making Ethiopia more democratic and less authoritarian. Still, there have been numerous violent incidents since Abiy's appointment and in 2020 and 2021 there has been a rise in attacks and massacres in several parts of Ethiopia. Ethnicity is a central factor in many of these conflicts.

In Ethiopia, the state ascribes ethnicity to people and the intensification of ethnic conflict can partly be traced back to the implementation of ethnic federalism in the 1990s. Through ethnic federalism, individuals' identities and group belonging are tied to specific regions of the country. My interlocutors who originated from the Tigray region predominantly considered themselves to be Tigrayans. Robel, who lived in Adigrat and had been a soldier for the TPLF at the end of the civil war, told me: 'My ethnicity is Tigrayan. Both my parents are Tigrayan.' This understanding of ethnicity resembles the government's discourse, but also differs from the official approach which classifies a person's ethnicity based only upon the father's ethnic background. Many referred to both parents to clarify their ethnic background, as Mehari did: 'My ethnicity is Tigrayan, but I can say I'm half Irob because my mother is Irob. On my ID card it says Tigrayan because my father is Tigrayan.' Tigrayan interlocutors generally adhered to the official categorisation, but the reflection by some on their mother's background suggests that the gender bias in the classification system did not always completely reflect their sense of ethnicity.

Among people who originated from outside of the Tigray region, it was more common to contest the EPRDF government's formal designation of ethnicity. Rather than referring to their ascribed ethnicity, several non-Tigrayans primarily spoke about themselves as 'Ethiopian.' Aster, a 21-year-old, was born in the countryside to parents of Gurage origin, but had lived most of her life in Addis Ababa. She had recently started a university degree in accounting at Aksum University in the Tigray region and responded to my question about her ethnicity by stating:

Aster: I'm Ethiopian.
Markus: OK, but what does it say on your ID card?
Aster: It says Gurage, but I don't think like that. I only think of myself as Ethiopian.

There were also non-Tigrayans who felt strongly about their ethnicity and placed it above national belonging, but ethnicity is not necessarily the primary source of group identity among young Ethiopians living in ethnically diverse urban centres (Mains 2012; Di Nunzio 2017). Like them, Aster did not consider ethnicity to be central to her identity and rejected the official group belonging stated in her identity card. Aster and other non-Tigrayan interlocutors who diverged from the government's discourse by emphasising nationality over ethnicity highlight that people's ways of identifying and presenting themselves varied. This discrepancy between how the state ascribes ethnicity and individuals' use of different categories makes it clear that the state cannot fully control meanings of ethnicity. Still, national policies and political contestations over power influence how people perceive ethnicity as well as encounters between people from different backgrounds.

As the quotes that opened this chapter indicate, since 1991, it was a well-established narrative that the government allocated disproportionate resources to the Tigray region and that individuals of Tigrayan ethnicity benefitted unfairly from the EPRDF political power structure. Perceptions of ethnicity-based inequality and Tigrayan advantage were common in Addis Ababa and underpinned the wider opposition to the regime in different parts of Ethiopia. Even as the government's designation of ethnicity was contested, many referred to Tigrayans as a distinct ethnic group. Yet representations of Tigrayans as a privileged group draw upon the same problematic assumption that the government employs in its rigid and fixed approach to ethnicity and overlooks the inequalities and differing identities among people from and in Tigray.

The varied and sometimes opposing views of the importance of ethnicity, and how it relates to individual and group privilege, raise questions about how ethnicity provides a lens on class and vice versa. Ortner (1998) identified two trends in studies of the relationship between ethnicity and class in the United States; the first is to treat ethnicity as the primary social category and ignore class completely, and the second approach is to approach the class as the economic aspect of determining people's life chances and ethnicity as a matter of prejudice and discrimination. Because of this, popular discourses and academic analyses of privilege, power, poverty and inequality have often focused upon ethnicity rather than class, hiding the class dimensions behind ethnicity (Ortner 1998). This point is relevant for understanding the relationship between ethnicity and class in other parts of the world; as Comaroff and Comaroff (1992, 59) have suggested, in many people's experiences ethnicity appears to determine an individual's status. Ethnicity impacts access to education and employment in many parts of the world and class positions sometimes emerge out of ascriptive differences (Lentz 2020), such as in some South American countries where the middle class is predominantly white (O'Dougherty 2002; Garguin 2007) and in South Africa where the colour bar determined black people's positions (Kuper 1965; Seekings 2009). Such perceptions and experiences contribute to make ethnicity a force with implications for the social world, while concealing the role of class.

This tendency to focus on ethnicity over class applies also in Ethiopia. The country has a feudal history as well as a revolutionary discourse of class, but the political system of ethnic federalism has contributed to making the ethnic discourse hegemonic. Many studies consequently place ethnicity at the centre of analysis (see e.g. Tronvoll 2009). Ethnic relations are central in many aspects of people's lives, though there is also value in analysing contemporary social relations through the lens of class. In this chapter, I look at how meanings of ethnicity change through urban-to-urban migration, with a view to developing a more nuanced understanding of the formation of a middle class in Ethiopia. I centre my attention on what happens when individuals migrate outside their designated ethnic territories, and, more specifically, I consider the experiences of ethnic diversity among Tigrayans who migrate for university studies and employment. Like Mains and Kinfu's (2016) study of how road construction materialises the politics of ethnicity in Hawassa in southern Ethiopia, the focus here is on the social outcomes of a politicised discourse around ethnicity (Breines 2020), which leads me to analyse how the contestations over ethnic inequalities enabled my interlocutors to find new ways of representing their identity as Tigrayans.

Disputed Ethnicity

Ethnicity is a contentious issue across the world. It is a concept that is often applied to explore the formation of individual identities and groups and its use is growing with the increased focus on international migration, globalisation and transnationalism. Appadurai (2006, 51) identifies a recurrent pattern across the world where the existence of a group 'defined as a we' is portrayed as being under threat by other social groups. To analyse the politics of ethnoracial categories, ethnonationalism and violence, he emphasises how 'anxiety of incompleteness' generates predatory identities, where majorities contest minorities' place in nations as a whole (Appadurai 2006, 8). A decade earlier, he coined the term 'ethnoscape' to describe how intensifying migration changes the landscape of social relations as well as national politics (Appadurai 1996, 33). In many contexts, ethnicity is a contentious issue because it is perceived to determine belonging and access to resources.

Ethnicity is particularly contentious in contexts where questions over belonging are used for political gain (Dorman et al. 2007). There are numerous examples of where ethnicity has been a factor in large-scale violence, such as in the former Yugoslavia and Rwanda in the early 1990s (Appadurai 2006), and more recently against the Rohingya in Myanmar (Prasse-Freeman 2017). Some scholars have considered the politicisation of ethnic identity and related violence as part of autochthony movements where the most authentic form of belonging is exclusive to those 'born from the earth itself,' and has been identified to arise in similar ways in countries like Cameroon and Belgium, despite their very different economic and social circumstances (Geschiere 2009). Such narratives about belonging inevitably create 'allochthons' who are claimed to not belong, thereby fuelling political conflict (Ceuppens and Geschiere 2005). However, it is not sufficient to equate autochthony movements to indigeneity, as conflicts over resources can partly be understood in relation to the increasing inequalities arising from global and local forms of neoliberal capitalism that seek to exclude some from wealth and power (Geschiere 2009). In many cases, ethnicity remains central in such processes. Ethnicity becomes politically and symbolically important in encounters between people from different groups (Eriksen 2010), but the ideas and negotiations of group belonging and identity also depend on the context and the circumstances of each encounter (Brubaker 2004). Autochthons rely on allochthons to define themselves in terms of characteristics that make them distinct from others and ethnicity, then, is not fixed but continuously negotiated (Barth 1969). In some cases, people have found less contentious and more entrepreneurial means of asserting ethnic identity, like the group of 'traditional' chiefs in South Africa who turned ethnicity into a business venture (Comaroff and Comaroff 2009). Such commoditisation serves as a reminder that people are not always caught up in the violent politics of ethnicity, but also reframe its meanings to their social or economic advantage.

With an increasing academic focus on migration and interactions between people from different backgrounds throughout the world, ethnicity remains a central concept because it speaks directly to fundamental concerns about how people understand themselves and others (Jenkins 2008). Much of the literature that examines the relationship between migration and ethnicity focuses on international migrants after arrival in host societies, especially in Europe and North America (see e.g. Dahinden 2008; Fleischmann et al. 2012; Somashekhar 2018). Considering the magnitude of migration within Africa (Flahaux and De Haas 2016), relatively little is known about how ethnic identities are reconstructed when people migrate within countries. Internal migration is a key factor in bringing together people from different ethnic groups and reshaping their relations in cities. As in other parts of the world, there has been an increase of autochthony movements in Africa and, in many cases, nation-building strategies have polarised people and facilitated the production of autochthons.

Ethnic Hierarchies in Ethiopia

How ethnicity is understood in contemporary Ethiopia is influenced by ideas of identity related to language, place of origin and culture. The history of highland domination over peoples in the surrounding lowlands has generated ethnicity-related conceptions of inequality. Rulers from Tigray and Amhara areas alternated in controlling parts of highland

Ethiopia until the end of the nineteenth century, but from the 1890s onwards Amhara rulers expanded their territories to dominate people in the lowlands, where assertions of highland superiority in terms of culture and religion were manifested in serfdom and enslavement of other populations as well as extraction of resources (Donham and James 1986). Whereas colonisers created multi-ethnic states across Africa, Ethiopia was built by expanding and incorporating peoples in the surrounding lowlands into an already existing state with a historical and cultural identity (Aalen 2011). People who spoke Amharic and originated from the highlands often controlled the means of production and exerted their power over people in the lowlands who spoke other languages, suggesting that ethnicity has been a factor of inequality from the early days of the Ethiopian nation-state (Aalen 2011). However, ethnicity was not perceived as fixed because people from other backgrounds could become Amhara by adopting Orthodox Christianity, the Amharic language and intermarriage, and thereby achieve state employment and political power (Donham 1986). Nevertheless, towards the end of the reign of Haile Selassie (1916–1974), ethnicity remained a central factor in social hierarchies and was intertwined with class in urban centres (Bjeren 1985).

The 1974 revolution arose partly in response to the contrasts between the excessive wealth concentrated in the ruling class and the deep poverty of the broader population. Many Ethiopians perceived the abolishment of the monarchy as an opportunity to transform the country into a modern state where economic and social inequalities could be reduced. Nevertheless, discrimination against many groups persisted. The Derg attempted to control the northern regions of Tigray and Eritrea through violence to an even greater extent than Haile Selassie, which led to further alienation of subjugated peasants and increasing opposition in the regions (Donham 2002). In the context of this suppression, the TPLF told Tigrayans that their poverty and hardship were an outcome of Amhara domination (Young 1998). The narratives of injustice and suffering contributed to Tigrayans beginning to see themselves as a separate group of people and to shape a Tigrayan ethnic identity that was used to mobilise against oppression (Donham 2002, 4). The notion of being Tigrayan was therefore largely shaped through the struggle against the Derg and Amhara subjugation.

The shift in political power in 1991 ended almost a century of Amhara dominance, but led to an intensification of the politicisation of ethnicity in Ethiopia. In order to legitimise its rule, the victorious EPRDF, led by the TPLF, had to show that it was less oppressive than its predecessors, could make the country prosperous and sustain peace in a multi-ethnic nation (Gagliardone 2014). The EPRDF responded to these challenges by reconfiguring the Ethiopian political system into ethnically based regions, a system which came to be known as 'ethnic federalism' (Abbink 2009). Ethnic federalism was, in part, an attempt to redress the historical hegemonic rule over marginalised groups in Ethiopia (Riggan 2011) and a means to give the different ethnic groups and regions more autonomy (Joireman 1997; Fiseha 2006), but political power remained largely centralised. Although ethnic federalism partially reflects popular perceptions of ethnic groups, or 'nationalities,' the formal designation of ethnicity contributed to territorialise ethnicity and ignored the long history of intermarriage and migration. In many respects, this political system has contributed to consolidate ideas of ethnicity as fixed and constrained the flexibility of ethnic belonging.

Ethnic federalism is based on a folk model, but ignores the continuous constructions, flexibility and performative aspects of ethnicity, and has real implications for how people enact their identities. The current ethnicity-based map of Ethiopia ascribes ethnic groups to specific regions of the country and makes ethnicity an official and permanent component of individual identity and group belonging. The rigid approach is manifested concretely in national identity cards. A person's ethnicity is determined solely based on his or her father's ethnic background, and from the perspective of the Ethiopian state, ethnicity is, together with other 'facts' of individual identity, such as name and date of birth, permanent and unchangeable. Ethnic federalism has turned ethnicity into a 'political asset' through provision of access to resources which, in combination with migration and increasing interactions with people from different backgrounds, has consolidated ideas of ethnic groups with distinct languages and cultural practices (Markakis 1998). Within a few years of the implementation of ethnic federalism, ethnicity became a very emotional issue for many Ethiopians (Abbink 1995) and ethnic conflict increased (Abbink 1998). This formalised politicisation has influenced how people understand and perform ethnicity, but also how they contest and seek to redefine the official meanings of ethnicity (Smith 2007).

Tigrayan politicians controlled the EPRDF government from 1991 until 2018, which influenced how Tigrayans were perceived by other Ethiopians and the dynamics in encounters between them. Many people in the lowlands saw the change in power dynamics and recent Tigrayan political domination as a continuation of the highland rule of the Amhara (Young 1996). The former associations of Tigray as a place ravaged by civil war, poverty and famine shifted towards it being seen as a favoured region where large proportions of Ethiopia's wealth came to be allocated. This perception, and suspicion of Tigrayans, was consolidated through the use of TPLF cadres to control federations and local governments as well as systematic subjugation, unlawful killings and arbitrary arrests of political opposition and ethnic groups in the lowlands (Jalata 2009; Tronvoll 2008, 2011). Tigrayans came to be seen as a new ruling elite, which attempted to monopolise political power and favoured the Tigray region by distributing more resources to that part of the country (Aalen 2011; Abbink 1995).

Ethnic tensions peaked when the opposition lost the 2005 election and claimed that they had been rigged. This led to demonstrations, with 195 protesters killed in Addis Ababa (Abbink 2006; Lyons 2006; Samatar 2005). Ethnic clashes have since occurred at regular intervals. People belonging to the largest ethnic groups in Ethiopia, Amhara and Oromo, as well as other backgrounds, regularly challenged Tigrayan minority rule through peaceful protests and armed resistance. In 2016, hundreds of people were killed in protests across Ethiopia (BBC 2017). In addition to violent clashes between security forces and protestors, there were news reports that properties associated with the Tigrayan ruling party were targeted in the city of Gondar and that many Tigrayans had fled north to Tigray (Yibeltal 2017). Over the years, the EPRDF government attempted to counter perceptions of Tigrayan dominance and privilege. The most obvious strategy was to not favour the Tigray region through official channels (Chanie 2007). Another way of promoting the idea of ethnic equality was through the moving from the earlier metaphors of nationhood based on highland 'culture' and Orthodox Christianity towards a more inclusive narrative of 'unity in diversity' (Orlowska 2013). By promoting the idea and claiming that all ethnic groups are equal, the government's position was that the Tigray region and individuals of Tigrayan ethnicity were not privileged over others.

The historical exploitation of different groups across the country as well as contemporary policies have contributed to make ethnicity a more contested issue in Ethiopia than in many postcolonial African states (Aalen 2011). At the same time as the politicisation and essentialisation of ethnicity intensified, opportunities for migration within Ethiopia have improved for many since 1991 (Kiros and White 2004). Ethiopians have the right to travel, live and work anywhere in the country, but because ethnicity is territorialised by the government's demarcation of regions, migration across regional boundaries effectively results in the movement of people from the territory to which their ethnicity is anchored into areas where they do not belong ethnically. Thus, any migration across regional boundaries results in contact with people from different ethnic groups. The 'territorial-administrative units' are based upon ethnicity and are used by local authorities to disadvantage people from other regions (Abbink 2011), which means that ethnic federalism shapes experiences and outcomes of migration. Migration in the highly politicised and conflict-laden ethnic context in Ethiopia and the subsequent social encounters situated in other ethnic power relations present individuals with shifting meanings of national and regional belonging, and for my interlocutors from Tigray this involved negotiation and reconsideration of what it meant to 'be Tigrayan.'

Essentialised Ethnicity at University

The large-scale expansion of higher education since 2000 and the government's mixing of the population on university campuses (Saint 2004) increased interactions between young people from different regions of Ethiopia. Tigray is the most homogenous region of Ethiopia (Mains and Kinfu 2016) and for many young people who had grown up in the region, going to university campuses in other regions was often their first experience of significant diversity. Tekle told me about when he joined Addis Ababa University in his early twenties:

> Until then, I had only been living in Korem [in Tigray]. At university, I met a lot of people from all over Ethiopia. In the dormitory, there were people who spoke other languages and had other religions. Some had other food customs and there were many different styles of clothing. Some were very clever, and some were fanatics [*akrari*]. There were many different people.

The opportunity to meet people from different backgrounds was highly valued among my interlocutors as it provided them with opportunities to widen their perspectives. Many had concerns about going to big cities for the first time, but Tekle's account of entering university and of living in a new environment on campus shows that he soon came to see the diversity as enriching.

Many interlocutors from Tigray spoke of the inherent value of living in diverse settings. Looking back at her undergraduate studies, Senait pointed out the value of being a student in other parts of the country:

> For my first degree in Bahir Dar I lived with people from different backgrounds. It was very nice getting to know many people from all over Ethiopia, sharing experiences and exchanging ideas. Now for the master's degree, I'm staying in an apartment by myself in Mekelle and many of the other students on my programme are from around here. It's not so different from living in Adigrat.

Through migration for higher education to other regions, people from Tigray became immersed in diverse contexts. Senait's fond memories of studying and living with students from all parts of Ethiopia had influenced her views on diversity, and she saw relationships across ethnic boundaries as valuable in themselves.

Despite my interlocutors' appreciation of getting to know people from different backgrounds, people coming together sometimes put them in difficult situations. In regions where perceptions of Tigrayan privilege prevailed, university students from the region occasionally faced prejudice, discrimination or violence because of their ethnicity. In relation to their familiarity with these prejudices and the widespread discontent with Tigrayan political power, they sometimes feared and hesitated to migrate to other parts of Ethiopia. However, it was difficult to turn down an opportunity to study at university because it could improve one's livelihood significantly. As a result, many saw no choice but to expose themselves to the dangers of living in other regions. Petros, who lived in Adigrat and worked for a local NGO, told me about his experience at Gondar University in the Amhara region: 'I feared racism before going to Gondar, and it happened to me on the eve of Easter. I was talking on my mobile phone and some guys on the street asked me "Why do you talk in Tigrinya? Why don't you speak Amharic?" Then they beat me and kicked me.' In Petros' view, he was attacked because he spoke Tigrinya in a region where the official language is Amharic. Petros became a target for contestation of Tigrayan dominance because of historical tensions between Tigrayans and Amharas in the Gondar area, but also because of the contemporary views of Tigrayans in the Amhara region. The perception of their ethnic privilege was a factor that impacted my Tigrayan interlocutors' safety outside Tigray.

Most of my research participants from Tigray experienced relatively minor incidents of violence and harassment during their university studies, but in some cases, the campuses became sites of full-fledged ethnic contestation. Tekle, who had initially embraced the diversity on campus, was one of the victims when men attacked a gathering of students in 2004:

> Some Oromo students who had joined OLF [Oromo Liberation Front] threw a grenade into the TV room when there were Tigrinya programmes on. One guy from Adigrat, one from Dessie and myself were injured, and one from around Debre Markos was killed. I had to stay in the Black Lion Hospital for one year after the attack. I still have some problems with my leg.

Because it happened at a time when there were mainly Tigrinya speakers watching TV, Tekle explained, the attack was related to discontent with the Tigrayan-dominated political leadership. The event also transformed Tekle's understanding of his own ethnicity and what it meant to be

Tigrayan. He had been aware of ethnic tensions prior to the attack, but this experience contrasted with his initial perceptions of ethnic diversity on arriving at Addis Ababa University. Through migration to other regions, my interlocutors became increasingly aware of the perceptions of Tigrayan privilege and under these circumstances, it became difficult to be 'neutral' in the politics of ethnicity. The impossibility of exiting the ethnic 'game' due to formally ascribed ethnicity made it a hotly contested topic in day-to-day interactions and could potentially lead to injury or even death. The violence on university campuses meant that the government's policy of mixing people from different backgrounds did not always generate common understanding; indeed, at times it contributed to turn campuses into battlegrounds.

In 2005, an election year, ethnic conflict escalated. Many Oromos contested the Tigrayan-dominated regime and their experiences of long-standing subjugation by highland-led governments. When it became clear that the EPRDF would remain in power, claims of rigging were made and violence intensified on university campuses. The police and security forces clamped down on protestors with force (Aalen and Tronvoll 2009). Around this time, students from Tigray who had migrated to towns and cities in other regions, such as Oromia, experienced discrimination, and violence. Mehari, who had studied at Jimma University in Oromia, told me about the conditions there: 'When I think of the campus I can only think of the racism. There was a lot of racism. Everybody was talking about Oromo, Amhara, Tigray.' As a Tigrayan in an environment where ethnicity has been particularly politicised in Ethiopia and at a time of strong emotions, Mehari got involved in conflicts with non-Tigrayans several times, including the police:

> Once I was going back to campus with a Tigrayan friend around 8pm, two policemen called us over and asked, "Where are you going?" We said we were going to the campus and they asked, "Where have you been?" It's none of their business where we've been and we got scared because we understood they wanted to bother us. We said we'd been with a friend or something, but they wanted a reason to beat us and asked for our ID cards. We showed it to them and there was no problem. They didn't have any reason, and then one of the policemen asked, "What is this hair?"

> while grabbing and pulling it at the same time. I had an Afro back then and answered "hair" and the policeman hit me with a flat hand. I hit him back with a flat hand and shouted "*wedi shermuta*!" [son of a bitch] to him and then it started. My friend attacked the other policeman, so we fought one-on-one. More policemen came and they pushed me to the ground and beat me with sticks. Then they pulled me by my legs through the mud and took me to prison. The police were racist. They didn't know us at all, and they wanted to beat us only because we spoke Tigrinya.

Tension between university students of all ethnicities and the police is common in Ethiopia and several of my interlocutors had experienced beatings by the police. Police violence can be understood in the broader contexts of the state exerting power over young menand enforcing conformity: Weiss (2005) observes how particular hairstyles have led to tense relations between young men and the police in Tanzania, and Mains (2012, 108) points to the power dynamics between the police and men in Ethiopia by giving an example of the police forcing a young man to cut his 'provocative' hairstyle. Mehari's ethnic origin could be identified through the language he spoke with his friend, but also by his hairstyle which was associated with TPLF rebel fighters arriving in central Ethiopia towards the end of the civil war. In Mehari's view, the attitude of the police and their use of force towards him and his friend was because they were Tigrayans in a part of Ethiopia where there was resistance against the Tigrayan-dominated regime.

The idea of Tigrayans as a privileged ethnic group was instrumental in my interlocutors' social relations during their university studies, especially at times of heightened political tension. The essentialised assumptions of their unique position acquainted them with a distinct set of meanings of being Tigrayan attributed to them by non-Tigrayans. Through migration to ethnically diverse university campuses, their ethnic affiliation with the Tigrayan-dominated EPRDF government familiarised them with discourses of ethnic inequality where their position became problematic because of their assumed social and economic privilege. This essentialised view and the coercive process of imposing specific attributes to their ethnicity (Bourgois and Schonberg 2007) entangled migrants in wider contestations over Tigrayan dominance as well as the distribution of resources and power in Ethiopia.

Asserting Ethnic Equality

After completing their degrees and returning to their places of origin, several of my interlocutors from Tigray pursued migration to urban centresin other parts of Ethiopia—despite their experiences of ethnic tension while at university elsewhere. These experiences were significantly less violent, but perceptions of Tigrayan privilege remained a source of tension in their social relations. In ethnically diverse urban spaces throughout Ethiopia, migrants reconstructed their Tigrayan ethnic identity in ways that were unique to those who were forced to respond to the ascribed meanings of their ethnicity and stereotyping by non-Tigrayans.

Even if many were aware of conceptions of Tigrayan privilege prior to migration, they became more exposed to these ideas when going to other parts of Ethiopia. Anbessa, aged thirty, told me about a headline he had seen in a newspaper in the early 2000s after migrating from Mekelle to Addis Ababa. It read *Ethiopian admto Mekellen mashebreq* ['Bleeding Ethiopia to decorate Mekelle']. The article claimed that resources were extracted from other parts of the country for the benefit of the Tigray region. The assumptions of 'ethnic nepotism' (Van den Berghe 1987), where Tigrayans benefitted because of their ethnicity, were explicit in printed media until the EPRDF-led government became more proactive about stifling critical voices following the contested 2005 election (Stremlau 2011). While such representations then became less common in the printed media, my Tigrayan interlocutors were aware of them and disagreed vehemently with the suggestion that they were favoured in any way. Anbessa had studied and worked in Addis Ababa since his late teens, apart from when he pursued a master's degree in Europe. He spoke fluent Amharic and had close friends from the Amhara and Oromia regions, though the ideas of Tigrayan privilege continued to be a concern for him:

> The ideas that Tigrayans are taking the resources and sending money to Tigray upsets me because it's not true. I've lived there and I know what's happening there. Maybe in federal governments there are more Tigrayan ministers than from other ethnic groups, but this is changing with time. In terms of budget there is a formula for allocating resources throughout the country based on the population and level of development in each region.

Anbessa continued to be concerned that people who had not actually been there and seen the conditions would believe the false portrayals.

It was in response to these narratives of inherent connections between Tigrayan ethnicity and privilege that my interlocutors had to position themselves in ethnically diverse urban centres. Their ethnicity as Tigrayans was often a topic of conversation. Elias had worked as doctor in Tigray before moving to Addis Ababa for further training and found that his ethnicity impacted how people related to him: 'Some people think differently about you because you are from Tigray. There are people who think that Tigray is being given advantages and that all the money goes to Tigray.' Such interactions made it evident to them that people from other backgrounds saw Tigrayans as a privileged group. In such situations, Elias felt compelled to contest the prejudices:

> For me there have been no problems because I'm from Tigray. My friends don't judge me for my ethnicity, but we often discuss it. Even today we discussed it, but in a reasonable way. I use my own experience to explain to my friends that I don't have any advantage over them. I tell them about my family's situation, how they live in the countryside and that my father was a freedom fighter. I try to make them understand that our situation is the same; we are doctors and get the same salary. I don't get one penny [*ammest santim*] more than them. There is a gap between people's understanding and reality. If they believe me when I say that the government is not carrying money to us, they understand the reality. Most of my friends accept my explanation.

Indeed, all my interlocutors from Tigray denied having ever experienced any favourable treatment. It is less known in other parts of Ethiopia that in the 1990s, people in Tigray had faced difficulties under the new government, as widespread poverty, limited support, perpetuation of the former bureaucracy and demands to provide free labour made life in Tigray challenging (Young 1997). For many Tigrayans in rural areas, these conditions had changed little.

Even though many Tigrayans continued to live in poverty and in harsh environments (Hammond 2004), it was common among non-Tigrayans to see ethnic federalism as an instrument for Tigrayans to subjugate and take advantage of other Ethiopians. Hewan, 26, who had lived in Addis Ababa for five years found such perspectives problematic:

> Many people have the wrong impression of Tigray and think that Tigrayans live an easy life. They believe there are asphalt roads everywhere, lots of universities and factories in Tigray and that Tigrayans get support from the government because the prime minister was from Tigray. It's not like that; in Tigray there are rich people and there are poor people.

The differences in perceptions of the relationship between state power and privilege illustrate that people's conceptualisations of how ethnicity intersects with hierarchical relations to some extent depends on their own ethnic identity. Tigrayan interlocutors who had migrated outside the Tigray region were familiar with the perceptions of their privilege and drew on their own experiences to problematise the claims that they benefited from their ethnic affiliation to the Tigrayan-led government.

The history of Tigrayan ethnic mobilisation during the civil war and the political system of ethnic federalism contributed to how people from the region sensed and narrated their ethnic belonging. The Tigrayans I engaged with construed their identity in terms of difference from other groups (see also Barth 1969), but at the same time, they maintained that there was no ethnicity-based system of inequality. By describing the prevalence of poverty in Tigray and pointing out that they faced the same opportunities and limitations as people from other ethnic groups in terms of employment conditions and salaries, they attempted to create a narrative of equality across ethnic boundaries. The doctor, Elias, and many others asserted their Tigrayan ethnicity when they contested prevailing ideas of their privilege in discussions about the facts of distribution of resources and inequality between ethnic groups, but these interactions with people who held different perspectives on ethnicity enhanced their capacity to deal with this contested issue and present their ethnicity in less contentious terms.

The different views on ethnic privilege and inequality did not mean that Tigrayans struggled to establish social relations with people from other ethnic groups. Rather, such relations were common among migrants who had a higher education and lived in urban centres outside Tigray. Hewan, for instance, had lived in the capital for five years and had a large social network:

> *Markus*: Do you have friends from other parts of Ethiopia?
>
> *Hewan*: Yes, I get along with people easily and my friends are from all over the country. The woman who called a few minutes ago is from Gondar. I have friends from Shashamene, Arba Minch and other places, though many are from Adigrat.
>
> *Markus*: And do you try to explain what the conditions are like in Tigray when you talk to them?
>
> *Hewan*: No, I don't want to discuss it with other people, it's better to be quiet when it comes up.

Essentialist ideas of ethnicity and the politics of Tigrayan otherness influenced my interlocutors' social interactions in everyday life. Even if Hewan attempted to stay out of such discussions, the perceptions of Tigrayan privilege made it difficult, if not impossible, to ignore ethnicity.

For migrants who had left Tigray and lived in other parts of the country, state-ascribed ethnicity and perceptions of ethnic belonging shaped their social relations. Their contested status as Tigrayans remained prominent in ethnically diverse settings—even if there was less violence in these contexts than at university campuses. By attempting to portray more nuanced perspectives on the conditions in Tigray, my interlocutors also asserted their own ethnic identity in opposition to narratives of their privilege. Elias tried to construct himself as an equal by challenging ideas of Tigrayan privilege, drawing on his own background and the employment and salary conditions he shared with his non-Tigrayan colleagues to demonstrate similarities. Hewan negotiated her Tigrayan identity more subtly than Elias and did not attempt to correct inaccurate perceptions, but also detailed the challenges her family in Adigrat faced to make it clear to me that she disagreed with the view that living conditions in Tigray were of a higher standard because of the region's ethnic affiliation to the EPRDF government. Gender may have been a factor in Hewan's less confrontational approach, but both strategies were responses to the politicised context where being Tigrayan was a source of tension. Both Hewan and Elias sought to present their ethnicity in a way that would enable them not only to avoid conflict, but also to maintain social relations with people from other backgrounds. As such, they attempted to de-politicise their ethnic identity as Tigrayans to be more compatible with other people in urban settings with diverse populations.

Essentialist ideas of ethnicity, claims of Tigrayan privilege, and the politics of Tigrayan otherness influenced interactions in daily life. 'My interlocutors from Tigray responded to others' perceptions of them as privileged by narrating and performing their own ethnicity in ways that could facilitate social relations across ethnic boundaries. Regardless of the strategies they chose to navigate this treacherous topic, they responded to the perceptions of being a group which benefited unjustly from government policies. Their ambiguous status as Tigrayans required them to re-imagine and develop their representations of their Tigrayan ethnicity to be more compatible in ethnically diverse settings. Frequent discussions about the distribution of resources and inequality between ethnic groups gave them practice in coping with a contested topic. Their growing capacity to expand their networks and maintain social relations with people from different backgrounds augmented their social capital compared to those Tigrayans who were less mobile and less skilled in coping with the contestations over their disputed ethnicity.

Transforming Tigrayan Identities

The political system of ethnic federalism has exacerbated ethnic tensions in Ethiopia. The EPRDF government politicised and essentialised ethnicity to an unprecedented degree by territorialising and ascribing ethnicity to individuals. The combination of this formalisation of ethnicity and intensifying internal migration contributed to construct migrants who crossed regional boundaries as allochthons, which in turn reinforced violent identity politics. The social processes surrounding ethnicity in Ethiopia resemble the ways in which 'anxiety of incompleteness' (Appadurai 2006) and autochthony movements (Geschiere 2009) are shaped in other parts of the world. The widespread perceptions of Tigrayans as privileged show the centrality of ethnicity in social hierarchies, but also that the politicisation of ethnicity by the government has contributed to the reification of ethnic belonging. The EPRDF government's systematic subjugation of political opposition and groups perceived to pose a threat to its rule (Jalata 2009; Tronvoll 2011) contributed to strengthen the ideas of an ethnicity-based system of inequality and Tigrayan privilege. Whereas Bayart (1993) suggested that African elites seek to control the state and 'eat' its resources, in the case of Ethiopia, people from other ethnic groups considered not only Tigrayan elites but the whole ethnic group to be consuming the wealth of the country.

Ethiopians' conceptualisations of ethnicity can be understood both in relation and in response to state categories, but the official ethnic classification of Ethiopians has constrained opportunities for developing identities that surmount ethnicity. Over the past decades, Tigrayan identity was effectively constituted and constructed by the opposition of other Ethiopians towards what they perceived to be Tigrayan hegemony. Rather than ethnicity being a political tool for the government to dominate non-Tigrayans, prevailing ideas of Tigrayan privilege and power made ethnicity a sensitive issue for people originating from Tigray. Tigrayans who migrated to other regions encountered face-to-face, essentialist and recurrent claims of their perceived privilege and the ethnicity-based system of inequality, which partly determined and restricted their capacity to claim non-ethnic identities in interactions with non-Tigrayans. In spite of the common perception that ethnic federalism advantaged Tigrayans, it actually contributed to essentialise Tigrayan ethnicity in ways that were to their disadvantage because of their shared ethnicity with the most powerful members of the EPRDF government. To my Tigrayan interlocutors, the political system was not beneficial to them; rather, it materialised distrust, resentment, discrimination and outright violence.

Tigrayan migrants gradually honed the skills needed to present their ethnic identity in response to conflicting meanings of their ethnicity in diverse social situations (this resembles Comaroff and Comaroff's [2009] point that some people alter how they present their own ethnicity in response to economic opportunities). Thus, ethnicity is both ascribed and achieved (Eriksen 2010), but individuals' presentation of their ethnic identities and the ways they construe others' identities also depends on policies and political contexts. The responses Tigrayans developed to the perceptions of their privilege illustrate that being Tigrayan was a negotiation of various perspectives—not a fixed attribute. Through experiences of migration to urban centres, they enhanced their capacities to interact with people from diverse ethnic backgrounds and developed strategies to respond to the claims of their privilege as Tigrayans. These experiences and skills made them distinct from less mobile people in Tigray, many of whom had relatively little experience of ethnic diversity (Image 6.1).

Image 6.1 Reaffirming Tigrayan identity with the celebration of *Mesqel* (Discovery of the True Cross), Adigrat

Rather than class shaping ethnicity, as Ortner (1998) and the Comaroffs (1992) suggested, my interlocutors' Tigrayan ethnicity placed them into a class position that was both privileged and contested. In South Africa, for example, black people are always subject to a racialised social hierarchy (Ndlovu 2020), but in Ethiopia, it seems to be other way around as Tigrayans had come to be seen as a separate class defined by ethnicity. While there was a class dimension in the essentialist representations and perceptions of Tigrayan privilege, my interlocutors' negation of ethnicity-based privilege and assertion of equality suggests that ethnicity did not determine class. Social distinctions were shaped through their capacity to establish and maintain social relations and avoid conflict despite essentialised ideas about their ethnicity-based privilege. In this context, then, class relations were not only shaped through ethnic privilege and inequality, but also by people developing the skills needed to adapt how they presented their Tigrayan identities under conditions of ethnic diversity.

In previous chapters, I focused on how material and symbolic capital could be increased through urban-to-urban migration and how those processes contributed to the formation of a middle class in Ethiopia. In this chapter I have shown that the Ethiopian discourse of ethnicity combined with the well-established ideas of Tigrayan dominance and privilege portray Tigrayans as a separate class, demonstrating that ethnicity is another factor in social hierarchies. How migrants navigated conflicting perspectives on the relationship between ethnicity and inequality in social interactions has revealed another way in which internal migration shaped knowledge, practices and values. My interlocutors' capacity to manage ethnic relations points to another dimension of how the social processes surrounding migration made them distinct and contributed to forming a group with shared skills in negotiating their Tigrayan ethnicity. By going beyond material wealth, the status of education and the engagement with modernity, this chapter has brought forward yet another factor that contributes to make urban-to-urban migrants distinct from others.

References

Aalen, Lovise. 2011. *The Politics of Ethnicity in Ethiopia: Actors, Power and Mobilisation under Ethnic Federalism*. Leiden; Boston: Brill.

Aalen, Lovise, and Kjetil Tronvoll. 2009. "The End of Democracy? Curtailing Political and Civil Rights in Ethiopia." *Review of African Political Economy* 36 (120): 193–207.

Abbink, Jon. 1995. Breaking and Making the State: The Dynamics of Ethnic Democracy in Ethiopia. *Journal of Contemporary African Studies* 13: 149–163.

Abbink, Jon. 1998. New Configurations of Ethiopian Ethnicity: The Challenge of the South. *Northeast African Studies* 5 (1): 59–81.

———. 2006. Discomfiture of Democracy? The 2005 Election Crisis in Ethiopia and Its Aftermath. *African Affairs* 105 (419): 173–199.

———. 2009. The Ethiopian Second Republic and the Fragile 'Social Contract.' *Africa Spectrum* 44 (2): 3–28.

———. 2011. Ethnic-Based Federalism and Ethnicity in Ethiopia: Reassessing the Experiment after 20 Years. *Journal of Eastern African Studies* 5 (4): 596–618.

———. 2017. *A Decade of Ethiopia: Politics, Economy and Society, 2004–2016*. A Decade of ... Series. Leiden ; Boston: Brill.

Appadurai, Arjun. 1996. *Modernity at Large: Cultural Dimensions of Globalization*. Minneapolis, MN: University of Minnesota Press.

———. 2006. *Fear of Small Numbers: An Essay on the Geography of Anger*. Durham and London: Duke University Press.

Barth, Fredrik. 1969. "Introduction." In *Ethnic Groups and Boundaries: The Social Organization of Culture Difference*, 9–38. Bergen; London: Universitetsforlaget; Allen & Unwin.

Bayart, J.-F. 1993. *The State in Africa: The Politics of the Belly*. London: Longman.

BBC. 2017. "Ethiopia Rights Body: 'More than 600 Protest Deaths.'" 2017. https://www.bbc.co.uk/news/world-africa-39619979.

Bjeren, Gunilla. 1985. *Migration to Shashemene: Ethnicity, Gender and Occupation in Urban Ethiopia*. Uppsala, Sweden: Scandinavian Institute of African Studies.

Bourgois, P., and J. Schonberg. 2007. Ethnic Dimensions of Habitus among Homeless Heroin Injectors. *Ethnography* 8 (1): 7–31.

Breines, Markus Roos. 2020. Ethnicity across Regional Boundaries: Migration and the Politics of Inequality in Ethiopia. *Journal of Ethnic and Migration Studies* 46 (14): 3335–3351. https://doi.org/10.1080/1369183X.2019.1577724.

Brubaker, Rogers. 2004. *Ethnicity without Groups*. Cambridge: Harvard University Press.

Ceuppens, Bambi, and Peter Geschiere. 2005. Autochthony: Local or Global? New Modes in the Struggle Over Citizenship and Belonging in Africa and Europe. *Annual Review of Anthropology* 34: 385–407.

Chanie, Paulos. 2007. Clientelism and Ethiopia's Post-1991 Decentralisation. *The Journal of Modern African Studies* 45 (3): 355–384.

Comaroff, John L., and Jean Comaroff. 1992. *Ethnography and the Historical Imagination*. Boulder, Colorado; Oxford: Westview Press.

———. 2009. *Ethnicity, Inc*. Chicago: University of Chicago Press.

Dahinden, Janine. 2008. Deconstructing Mythological Foundations of Ethnic Identities and Ethnic Group Formation: Albanian-Speaking and New Armenian Immigrants in Switzerland. *Journal of Ethnic and Migration Studies* 34 (1): 55–76.

Di Nunzio, Marco. 2017. "Marginality as a Politics of Limited Entitlements: Street Life and the Dilemma of Inclusion in Urban Ethiopia." *American Ethnologist* 44 (1): 91–103.

Donham, Donald L. 1986. Old Abyssinia and the New Ethiopian Empire. In *The Southern Marches of Imperial Ethiopia: Essays in History & Social Anthropology*, edited by Wendy James and Donald L. Donham, 3–48. Oxford: James Currey.

———. 2002. "Introduction." In *Remapping Ethiopia: Socialism & After*, edited by Wendy James, Eisei Kurimoto, Donald L. Donham, and Alessandro Triulzi, 1–7. Oxford, England; Addis Ababa; Athens: Ohio University Press.

Donham, Donald L., and Wendy James, eds. 1986. *The Southern Marches of Imperial Ethiopia: Essays in History & Social Anthropology*. Cambridge: Cambridge University Press.

Dorman, Sara, Daniel Hammett, and Paul Nugent, eds. 2007. *Making Nations, Creating Strangers: States and Citizenship in Africa*. African Social Studies Series 16. Leiden: Brill.

Eriksen, Thomas Hylland. 2010. *Ethnicity and Nationalism: Anthropological Perspectives*, 3rd ed. London and New York: Pluto Press.

Fiseha, Assefa. 2006. Theory Versus Practice in the Implementation of Ethiopia's Ethnic Federalism. In *Ethnic Federalism: The Ethiopian Experience in Comparative Perspective*, edited by David Turton, 131–164. Oxford: James Currey.

Flahaux, Marie-Laurence., and Hein De Haas. 2016. African Migration: Trends, Patterns, Drivers. *Comparative Migration Studies* 4 (1): 1.

Fleischmann, Fenella, Karen Phalet, Patrick Deboosere, and Karel Neels. 2012. Comparing Concepts of Ethnicity in Ethnic Composition Measures: Local Community Contexts and the Educational Attainment of the Second Generation in Belgium. *Journal of Ethnic and Migration Studies* 38 (10): 1513–1531.

Gagliardone, Iginio. 2014. New Media and the Developmental State in Ethiopia. *African Affairs* 113 (451): 279–299.

Garguin, Enrique. 2007. 'Los Argentinos Descendemos de Los Barcos': The Racial Articulation of Middle Class Identity in Argentina (1920–1960). *Latin American and Caribbean Ethnic Studies* 2 (2): 161–184.

Geschiere, Peter. 2009. *The Perils of Belonging: Autochthony, Citizenship, and Exclusion in Africa and Europe*. Chicago: University of Chicago Press.

Hammond, Laura. 2004. *This Place Will Become Home: Refugee Repatriation to Ethiopia*. N.Y.; London: Cornell University Press.

Jalata, A. 2009. "Being in and out of Africa: The Impact of Duality of Ethiopianism." *Journal of Black Studies* 40 (2): 189–214.

Jenkins, Richard. 2008. *Rethinking Ethnicity*, 2nd ed. Thousand Oaks, CA: Sage Publications.

Joireman, Sandra Fullerton. 1997. Opposition Politics and Ethnicity in Ethiopia: We Will All Go Down Together. *The Journal of Modern African Studies* 35: 387–407.

Kiros, Gebre-Egzbiabher., and Michael J. White. 2004. Migration, Community Context, and Child Immunization in Ethiopia. *Social Science & Medicine* 59 (12): 2603–2616.

Kuper, Leo. 1965. *An African Bourgeoisie: Race, Class, and Politics in South Africa*, Vol. 142. Yale University Press.

Lentz, Carola. 2020. Doing Being Middle-Class in the Global South: Comparative Perspectives and Conceptual Challenges. *Africa* 90 (3): 439–469. https://doi.org/10.1017/S0001972020000029.

Lyons, Terrence. 2006. Ethiopia in 2005: The Beginning of a Transition? *CSIS Africa Notes* 25 (January): 1–8.

Mains, Daniel. 2012. *Hope Is Cut: Youth, Unemployment, and the Future in Urban Ethiopia*. Philadelphia: Temple University Press.

Mains, Daniel, and Eshetayehu Kinfu. 2016. Making the City of Nations and Nationalities: The Politics of Ethnicity and Roads in Hawassa, Ethiopia. *The Journal of Modern African Studies* 54 (04): 645–669.

Markakis, John. 1998. "The Politics of Identity: The Case of the Gurage in Ethiopia." In *Ethnicity and the State in Eastern Africa*, edited by Mohamed Abdel Rahim M Salih and John Markakis, 127–46. Uppsala, Sweden: Nordiska Afrikainstitutet.

Ndlovu, Thabisani. 2020. Shuttling between the Suburbs and the Township: The New Black Middle Class(Es) Negotiating Class and Post-Apartheid Blackness in South Africa. *Africa* 90 (3): 568–586. https://doi.org/10.1017/S000197202000008X.

O'Dougherty, Maureen. 2002. *Consumption Intensified: The Politics of Middle-Class Daily Life in Brazil*. Duke University Press.

Orlowska, Izabela. 2013. Forging a Nation: The Ethiopian Millennium Celebration and the Multiethnic State. *Nations and Nationalism* 19 (2): 296–316.

Ortner, Sherry B. 1998. Identities: The Hidden Life of Class. *Journal of Anthropological Research* 54 (1): 1–17.

Prasse-Freeman, Elliott. 2017. The Rohingya Crisis. *Anthropology Today* 33 (6): 1–2. https://doi.org/10.1111/1467-8322.12389.

Riggan, Jennifer. 2011. "In Between Nations: Ethiopian-Born Eritreans, Liminality, and War." *PoLAR: Political and Legal Anthropology Review* 34 (1): 131–54.

Saint, William. 2004. Higher Education in Ethiopia: The Vision and Its Challenges. *Journal of Higher Education in Africa/revue De L'enseignement Supérieur En Afrique* 2 (3): 83–113.

Samatar, Abdi Ismail. 2005. The Ethiopian Election of 2005: A Bombshell & Turning Point? *Review of African Political Economy* 32 (104/105): 466–473.

Seekings, Jeremy. 2009. The Rise and Fall of the Weberian Analysis of Class in South Africa Between 1949 and the Early 1970s. *Journal of Southern African Studies* 35 (4): 865–881.

Smith, Lahra. 2007. Voting for an Ethnic Identity: Procedural and Institutional Responses to Ethnic Conflict in Ethiopia. *The Journal of Modern African Studies* 45 (4): 565–594.

Somashekhar, Mahesh. 2018. "Ethnic Economies in the Age of Retail Chains: Comparing the Presence of Chain-Affiliated and Independently Owned Ethnic Restaurants in Ethnic Neighbourhoods." *Journal of Ethnic and Migration Studies*.

Stremlau, N. 2011. The Press and the Political Restructuring of Ethiopia. *Journal of Eastern African Studies* 5 (4): 716–732.

Tronvoll, Kjetil. 2008. Human Rights Violations in Federal Ethiopia: When Ethnic Identity Is a Political Stigma. *International Journal on Minority and Group Rights* 15 (1): 49–79.

———. 2009. *War & the Politics of Identity in Ethiopia: Making Enemies & Allies in the Horn of Africa*. Woodbridge, Suffolk; Rochester, NY: James Currey.

———. 2011. "Briefing: The Ethiopian 2010 Federal and Regional Elections: Re-establishing the One-Party State." *African Affairs* 110/438: 121–36.

Van den Berghe, P.L. 1987. *The Ethnic Phenomenon*. Santa Barbara, California: ABC-CLIO.

Weiss, B. 2005. "The Barber in Pain: Consciousness, Affliction & Alterity in Urban East Africa." In *Makers & Breakers: Children and Youth in Postcolonial Africa*, edited by F De Boeck and A Honwana, 102–20. Oxford: James Currey.

Yibeltal, Kalkidan. 2017. "Ethiopia: Ethnic Nationalism and the Gondar Protests." AlJazeera,. 2017. https://www.aljazeera.com/indepth/features/2017/01/ethiopia-ethnic-nationalism-gondar-protests-170102081805528.html.

Young, John. 1996. "Ethnicity and Power in Ethiopia." *Review of African Political Economy* 23 (70): 531–42.

———. 1997. "Development and Change in Post-Revolutionary Tigray." *Journal of Modern African Studies* 35 (1): 81–99.

———. 1998. "Regionalism and Democracy in Ethiopia." *Third World Quarterly* 19 (2): 191–204.

7

A Middle Class Rooted in Urban-to-Urban Migration

An Unconscious Unity of Class

This book began on the Selam Bus. On the face of it, such journeys are physical movements from one location to another, but migration in Ethiopia is also influenced by social and economic inequalities, as well as by powerful ideologies and discourses of development and progress. As the Selam Bus was the most expensive overland travel option, there was an economic dimension to these journeys which distinguished its passengers from people who used cheaper or more expensive forms of transport. Economic categorisations of classes can, to some extent, provide a point of comparison between class relations in different countries (Mercer and Lemanski 2020) but do not facilitate analysis of the social processes through which distinctions are produced in each context. Rather than attempting to determine people's inclusion in, or exclusion from, a middle class in terms of their possession and use of economic capital, my ethnography has unpacked how urban-to-urban migration shapes distinct knowledge, practices and values. Each of my interlocutors followed separate trajectories, but shared experiences, perspectives and

M. R. Breines, *Becoming Middle Class*,
Globalization, Urbanization and Development in Africa,
https://doi.org/10.1007/978-981-16-3537-3_7

individual transformations as a result of their higher education studies and employment in different urban centres. Instead of the commonalities in their strategies and practices generating local class vocabularies or a 'class consciousness' of middle-class belonging, they shared an 'unconscious unity of class' (Bourdieu 1984, 77).

The concept of 'middle class' has often been used in reifying and deterministic ways (Lentz 2020; Skeggs 2015). Several scholars have pointed out that it is especially difficult to research the middle classes (Heiman, Freeman, and Liechty 2012; Liechty 2003; Wacquant 1991). While the processes that form class relations may not always be apparent, they can still be fundamental in creating loosely defined groups. In the preceding chapters, I have demonstrated the value of anthropological methods in identifying people's lived experience of migration and the related social processes through which distinctions emerge. The purpose of this ethnography is not to pin down specific characteristics of *the* Ethiopian middle class, but to identify the temporal, contentious and unpredictable processes that led to the formation of *a* middle class in a specific context.

My focus on the formation of a middle class is not an attempt to idealise the realities of people's lives. There are clearly many people living in poverty in Ethiopia (Heinonen 2013; Nunzio 2019), but in recent years it has become increasingly evident that there are also many professionals across urban Africa (Spronk 2012, 2020; Hull 2020) and some anthropologists have turned their attention from marginalised people and lower classes to middle classes (Heiman et al. 2012). Alongside economic growth and a growing interest in African middle classes, scholars have problematised the economic classifications (Melber 2016) and instead focus on the political and processual aspects of class relations (Sumich 2018). Still, further research on the lives of those who are at the forefront of African modernities can provide more nuanced understandings of the relational dimensions of contemporary class formation across the continent.

Through my examination of people who live 'in between' and how they responded to opportunities and constraints, I have suggested that there is a wider diversity of social realities in Ethiopia than what is commonly portrayed. Engagement with urban-to-urban migration informed and transformed individuals as it enhanced their access to new lifestyles and diversity, as well as to well-paid employment, and gave them skills in coping with tensions related to their ethnicity. Urban-to-urban migration became a site that brought together a distinctive set of features: practices involving higher education, consumption, private-sector employment; knowledge of life in other urban centres, modernity, ethnic tensions, values of sharing and in terms of what progress meant to them. Social hierarchies are entangled in the political, economic and social structures, but these often subtle transformations shaped the distinctions that united them by being different from international migrants and those who did not migrate, and constituted a process through which an unconscious unity of a middle class was produced.

Distinctions and Commonalities

The social, economic and material changes that have taken place in Ethiopia over the past decades influenced my interlocutors' perceptions of progress. They saw development as a process of national improvement which could have direct consequences for their livelihoods. These processes were perceived to primarily take place in big cities and the term 'access' was used to refer to conditions where they would be able to pursue more fulfilling lives. Similarly, the more diverse composition of the population in bigger cities, such as Addis Ababa, created conditions for them to expand their networks and thereby deepen their knowledge of the world; combined with their engagement with objects and relations in a wider system of value and meaning, this in turn made them distinct from people with less or other experiences of migration.

My interlocutors' decision to remain in Ethiopia reflected the possibilities in other urban centres for improving their lives in ways that, to them, meant progress. Internal migration was integral to the processes of higher education and subsequent career development as it brought people into new geographical and social spaces where they could progress. While international migration could generate higher incomes for some time, the poor working conditions abroad and perceived arrogance of returnees made it an unattractive option. Opportunities to migrate within Ethiopia were embedded in existing inequalities and the experiences of those who moved between cities and obtained higher education generated behaviours, tastes and consumption patterns that conferred on them the status of an educated person (*yetemare saw*). Their educational credentials, employment patterns and increasing wealth generated commonalities among urban-to-urban migrants and distinguished them from those who did not pursue this form of migration.

Migration trajectories are often related to class position, but there is no predetermined relationship between physical and social mobility. Many of the young women and men who face poor prospects in African countries are attracted to international migration (Graw and Schielke 2012), but through my focus on the social processes related to urban-to-urban migration in Ethiopia, I have shown that international migration is not the most attractive option for everyone and that people's conceptualisations of progress influence their migration choices. The EPRDF government's approach to development influenced how some people perceived their chances to improve their lives within the country, such as through the expansion of higher education and the construction and upgrade of infrastructure. My interlocutors' preference for migration between urban centres stemmed from their perceptions of how social change and development in such places could affect their lives, and their migration histories and recurrent movements between cities was a response to contemporary, and sometimes temporary, opportunities for employment and prosperity, as well as the legal, financial and social constraints on migration abroad. Nevertheless, people migrated for their own reasons, to different places and for varying lengths of time, accentuating that migration can be frequent and unpredictable (King 2012). Recognising this complexity of migration, I have referred to urban-to-urban migration as the journeys between locations as well as a process that involves spending a substantial period of time, either temporary or permanent, in other urban centres.

These migrations and associated individual transformations occasionally created tensions between what was construed as a modern versus a traditional lifestyle. Because of the high cost of living and difficulties of transport in Addis Ababa, many struggled to live up to the expectations of maintaining social relations and providing support for family, relatives and friends, regardless of the access and diversity it offered. The economic difficulties and time constraints due to the long distances and heavy traffic led them to live very different social lives in the capital from those led in Adigrat. As a result, their seemingly individualistic lifestyles in bigger cities were subject to criticism, especially when they were unable to share economic capital and fulfil reciprocal relations. This in turn constrained their sense of progress.

Moreover, ethnic tensions pervaded many social relations. Migration to other regions and exposure to conflicting perspectives on the relationship between ethnicity and inequality entangled my interlocutors in contestations over Tigrayan dominance and the national distribution of resources and power, which in turn gave them no option but to find new ways to present their ethnic identities as Tigrayans. Many found the persistent focus on their ethnicity in social relations challenging, though, at the same time, their experiences of encounters with people from diverse ethnic backgrounds expanded their networks and enhanced their capacity to navigate relationships across ethnic boundaries, which contributed to distinguish them from people who lived in ethnically more homogenous areas.

The distinctions that arose through this group's engagement in urban-to-urban migration point to the social, cultural and relational dimensions, as well as the economic expressions, of the inequalities that underlie the formation of a middle class. Class relations are embedded in historical and social contexts (Mercer and Lemanski 2020) in Ethiopia, but Nallet (2015) finds that there is no local terminology for 'middle class' and suggests that it is not suitable to impose this concept on the Ethiopian context because it does not sufficiently reflect the more complex social realities she observed. However, the analysis of a middle class does not need to reflect exact local vocabulary or attempt to unpack class relations in all their complexity. Instead, my focus is on the formation of a group that is not a permanent or tangible entity, but one whose members share certain characteristics and can be differentiated from others. There may well be a range of other groups that could be described as being middle class where the individuals share other characteristics, pursue different lifestyles and possess more or less wealth, but the concept of 'middle class' is still valuable for analysing how social hierarchies are shaped through the production of commonalities and distinctions, both in the short term and in the longer run.

Continuing Trajectories

After the fieldwork for this research was completed, I returned to Ethiopia several times. My continued engagement with friends and interlocutors has given me insights into how their lives unfolded over the subsequent years. Some continued migrating between cities at regular intervals and others settled down. These longer trajectories point to the shifting meanings of progress depending on how their careers and opportunities changed over time. I will here focus on two post-fieldwork narratives.

The continued anti-Tigrayan sentiment in parts of Ethiopia made travel outside of Tigray less appealing to Mehari and he has remained in Adigrat. When I visited Ethiopia in 2015, he was working full-time as a trekking guide in the mountains. He was still living in his parents' compound, but the room where we had stayed together was now part of the residence of Kidane, an elder brother of Mehari who had recently returned to Adigrat with his family after living in another city in Tigray for more than a decade. The tenants who had previously lived in small, one-room houses in the compound had been told to leave to make space for Kidane to construct an extension of the house for his family. Mehari had moved into a room with Kidisti, his younger sister, in the same building as their parents. Kidisti had returned to Adigrat after completing her bachelor's degree from Bahir Dar University and had obtained temporary employment laying cobblestones while trying to find more rewarding and better-paid employment. After I had spent a few days in Adigrat, I hired Mehari as a research assistant to travel with me to Shire in western Tigray to help me conduct research for an international organisation. Mehari arranged to meet up with a friend he had studied with about a decade earlier and who was currently teaching at the Shire branch of Aksum University. By coincidence, during our stay we also encountered two other people on this trip whom Mehari knew from his time at Jimma University, illustrating to me how he had expanded his networks and social capital during his university studies.

When I returned to Ethiopia in 2018, Mehari had started a restaurant. Kidisti was working there as a manager and ran the restaurant when Mehari took tourists trekking for several days. Mehari no longer lived in his parents' compound and instead rented a room about a hundred metres from the restaurant. As we sat on his bed (there were no chairs) reminiscing about the past, he pointed out that the large bed he had bought was much better than the thin mattress on the floor we used to sleep on in the past. During my brief stay in Adigrat, we went to visit his parents where Kidane had by now completed the construction of his house and his wife had expanded the garden and was growing vegetables. Mehari's restaurant and Kidane's large house suggest that they had been continuing to improve their financial situations. Such material changes were visible and easier for me to identify than the more subtle transformations in people's social relations that would require more time and research-focused conversations.

My next visit was in 2019 when I travelled to Adigrat to attend Mehari's wedding (Images 7.1 and 7.2). It was the first time my wife had the opportunity to visit Ethiopia and in the week prior to the wedding,

Image 7.1 Dancing and blessing the bride during a wedding, Adigrat

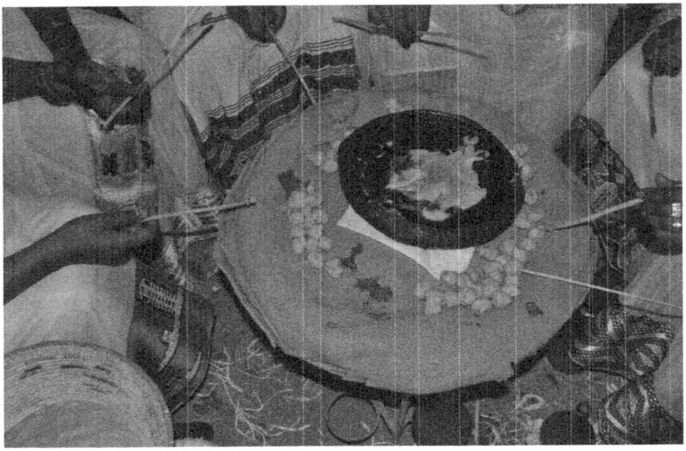

Image 7.2 Communal eating during a wedding, Adigrat

we went on two-day trek in the mountains outside Adigrat with Mehari's colleague. He was eagerly anticipating Mehari's wedding and so were the people working in the village where we spent the night, about a five-hour walk from Adigrat. It was clear to me that it would be a big wedding, with guests not only from Adigrat but also from nearby and more distant villages. By the time we returned to the city, several relatives of Mehari had arrived from Addis Ababa as well as rural and urban areas across Tigray. Many of them stayed with his parents and when I visited a few days before the wedding I could see that further changes had taken place in the compound. Mehari's older brother, Nebay, had recently got married and had started building a house for his family next to the others to prepare for a more permanent return to Adigrat. This was the first building to have two floors instead of one. Mehari's father had already arranged for plots of land for each of his children in the rural areas outside Adigrat, but it was not really an option for them to settle for a more rural lifestyle at this point in their lives. There was also a plot for Mehari in the compound, where he was planning to start constructing a house as soon as he earned enough money from his restaurant. He was optimistic about his business and envisaged that he would at least have started building and have a room for me to stay in the next time I visited.

Mehari's wedding was held on the street, covered by a tent, outside a new restaurant he had opened towards the end of 2018. His first restaurant was doing very well, but he told me that he had passed it on to Kidisti so she could have a business of her own. The new restaurant had been open for about eight months by the time I visited, but it was already popular. His wedding was just a few days away and Mehari was very busy with the large number of customers in the restaurant around midday and between 6 and 8 pm. Looking at him as he was sending orders to the kitchen and handing out hot dishes for the waiters to distribute to the tables, I thought about how different Mehari's life was from when I first met him in Addis Ababa in 2006. Back then, he went out drinking and dancing as often as he could and got into fights regularly. He had not been sure what to do with his life as he had not been able to complete his higher education degree because of the fragile situation at Jimma University at the time. He had continued the same kind of lifestyle for several years and his siblings had worried about him as they thought he lacked direction. But, over the last four or five years, he had gradually changed his behaviour and found stronger faith in Orthodox Christianity. Now that he was getting married and his wife-to-be was also working in the restaurant, he seemed to have found his place.

The trajectories of other interlocutors were similar, though with individual variations. In 2015, I met Tesfay several times for coffee and dinner in the Hayahulett neighbourhood where he was living in Addis Ababa. I was happy that he had been well enough to move to the capital and establish his own law firm (see Chapter 3), even with his heart condition. The money donated by a church organisation and his friends (see Chapter 5) had enabled him to travel to Thailand in 2013, but the doctors there advised against surgery because his heart condition was too precarious and there was a high risk of him dying during the procedure. When he returned to Ethiopia, he stayed with his aunt and uncle on the outskirts of Addis Ababa. A few days after his arrival, I went to visit him. Tesfay picked me up at the minibus stop as there were too many condominiums in the area for me to find the right one. The flat was on the fourth floor and he had to stop several times to catch his breath as we walked up the stairs. After a few weeks, however, he started feeling better and wanted to return to Wukro where he had his own place. We organised to fly to Mekelle together because Tesfay preferred not to travel alone in case something happened during the journey, and I was travelling to Adigrat to finalise my fieldwork there in any case.

I stayed in touch with Tesfay via Facebook after I returned to the United Kingdom, and was surprised when he told me a few months later that he felt back to normal. Tesfay explained that he had been treated with holy water (*tsebel*) and that this had helped a lot. The next time we met was in early 2018, but we only met once for dinner as I was in Addis Ababa for just two nights. Tesfay told me that his work was going well and that he was living with a woman and that they had recently had a child together. Even with the good news, he seemed somewhat subdued to me, but we did not have much time together and I was not able to figure out why. Tesfay passed away a few weeks later.

Tesfay, Mehari and others experienced significant changes in their lives both before and after my research. The differences between my interlocutors trajectories can partly be attributed to the socio-economic situation of their families as well as their individual aspirations and opportunities that arise. Tesfay's family remained in rural areas whereas Mehari and his brothers had been able to prosper partly because their father was a civil servant, with a regular income and access to influential networks, which gave them better chances in life (even though Mehari did not complete his higher education degree). The commonalities in the transformations in their lives, as well the lives of other interlocutors, can be attributed to their higher education as well as the opportunities and skills that they gained through migration between urban centres. As their continued progress shows, the middle-class formation I have described does not reach an end point; the negotiation of social status and position is a process, which continues throughout life.

Non-linear Upwards Social Mobility

Higher education can enhance individuals' material and symbolic capital but can nonetheless have limited impact on their actual social mobility. For Bourdieu (1984), cultural capital is internalised early in people's lives and this embodiment of their origin forms barriers to upward social mobility. This means that elites are in a better position to convert the symbolic capital of education into economic capital because their networks (social capital) will help them find well-paid employment. Analyses of people's possession and use of capital can be applied to understand social hierarchies in most, if not all, parts of the world, but the processes of differentiation are highly local. Bourdieu's focus was on hierarchies of taste in France in the 1960s and 1970s, and the ways in which people create distinctions between each other will inevitably be very different in other places half a century later.

My examination of middle-class formation has demonstrated that social hierarchies differ not only between countries but also between urban centres within Ethiopia. An increase in capital in one place does not necessarily carry the same value in other places. The analysis of how people change through migration and over time has demonstrated that their possession and use of capital is not static, which is an outcome both of their own progress and in response to the diverse interactions through which their relational positions in social hierarchies are situated. My interlocutors' experiences of higher education and obtaining employment changed their social relations and status, but in a place like Addis Ababa, they could still be perceived as backwards in some circles because of their social origin and lack of context-specific cultural capital. Even though cultural capital is foundational and tenacious compared to other forms of capital, people's status is highly dependent on the context and how they are perceived by others. The variations between places are evidence that there are not intrinsic values of practices that locate people in social hierarchies, but that these processes are relational and therefore also influenced by other factors, such as gender and ethnicity (Bennett et al. 2009). Also, the multitude of social compositions and diverse hierarchies that co-exist in bigger cities complicate class relations.

Consequently, I have not attempted to portray middle-class formation as a straightforward form of upwards social mobility. I have drawn on Bourdieu's (1984, 1986) insights into class and to demonstrate that people proactively pursued opportunities to improve their lives and experienced some degree of upwards social mobility through urban-to-urban migration. Some scholars have suggested that Bourdieu's work on class is excessively focused on the reproduction of the status quo and overlooks individual agency (Spronk 2018; Ortner 2003), whereas others have made the case that Bourdieu was well aware of people's efforts to achieve social mobility (Friedman and Savage 2017). In this book, I have highlighted my interlocutors' individual strategies and practices related to migration, which has demonstrated that they were actors in cultural production through which they enhanced their material, symbolic and social capital.

Yet I do not seek to portray this transformation as a form of upwards social mobility, wherein people simply move up a vertical line (Fig. 7.1). Even with these enhancements of capital, people's social origins (their cultural capital) constrained their social mobility—without merely reproducing their social positions. Their strategies, practices and individual experiences shifted their social relations, and therefore also their social positions. At the same time, however, their diverse statuses and the multiple power relations in which they were entangled in cannot be tagged to a vertical line. Instead, I suggest an alternative, less linear version of social hierarchies (Fig. 7.2). In this version, the vertical line is not straight as people's social positions on the scale are shifting and dependent on temporal and situational interactions and conditions. The scale cannot be fixed because it is slowly, but continuously, being reshaped (Friedman and Savage 2017). Considering these dynamics,

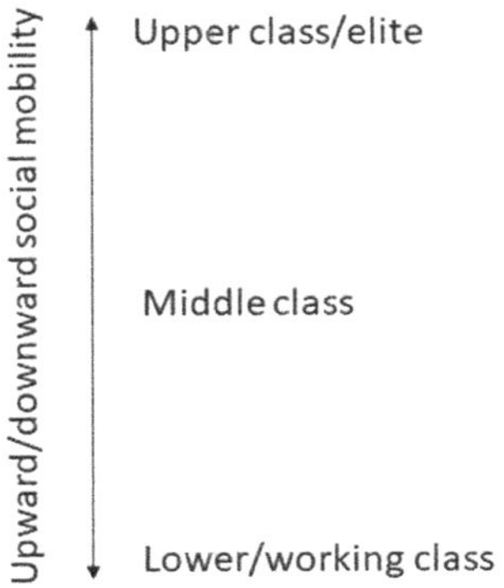

Fig. 7.1 Social mobility in a simplified depiction of social hierarchies

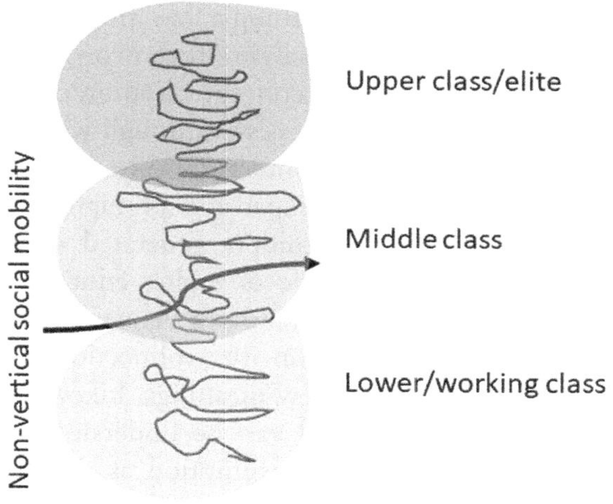

Fig. 7.2 An alternative depiction of social mobility. Here people cannot be easily tagged to specific positions on a vertical scale, but cross over different and overlapping positions depending on their possession of capital and location, and the various other factors that influence their positions in relation to others

the formation of the middle class in Ethiopia to which I have referred throughout this book can be illustrated by an arrow that is neither straight nor pointing directly upwards. This meandering line helps to reflect my interlocutors' ambiguous social mobility.

Despite the commonalities among migrants, their trajectories were not all the same. As shown in the cases of Mehari and Tesfay, individual circumstances impacted their opportunities and how their lives unfolded. The pace of upwards social mobility differed depending on people's success in obtaining employment and establishing their own businesses (see also Friedman and Savage 2017), meaning that the middle-class formation I have described does not rely on everyone following the same trajectories. Female interlocutors generally faced social and economic constraints to migration, which limited their possibilities for expanding their networks and achieving material gain, and slowed down their progress compared to men (Li, Savage, and Warde 2008)—highlighting that the temporalities of class relations are also gendered.

This ethnographic research in Ethiopia has shown that Bourdieu's work on capital can be applied to analyse African contexts, but also that such approaches can expand on the conceptualisation of capital through identification of the diverse social processes through which people create distinctions also in non-European contexts (see also Utsa 2014; Vazquez Maggio 2017). For instance, the expansion of higher education and introduction of cost-sharing in Ethiopia generated opportunities for more people to study, but the value of higher education degrees has also shifted with larger number of graduates. As new networks between people are created through migration, the connections that constitute social capital change and take on new meanings. Likewise, what constitutes material and symbolic capital can be understood in relation to localised patterns of conspicuous consumption as well as how people shift their use of objects, language and symbols for differentiation (Prieur and Savage 2013). Rather than working with predetermined conceptions of how to assess capital, analyses of the assets that serve as capital need to be explored in relation to the cultural constructions of legitimacy and power (Savage, Warde, and Devine 2005), which enables identification of how classes that are unique to each context emerge through the continuous production of distinctions.

In examining the social, cultural and relational processes surrounding migration in Adigrat and Addis Ababa, this book has focused on the formation of a middle class. Although internal migration has to some extent been out of the academic limelight in recent years, it continues to take new forms and meanings. By shifting the gaze back to the anthropological interest in the social implications of migration to urban centres, the value of taking into consideration the role of internal migration in contemporary class formations has been emphasised. Recent studies have proposed that insights into middle classes in Africa can offer help understand class in the rest of the world (Spronk 2018; Lentz 2020), and my analysis of the relationship between urban-to-urban migration and middle-class formation in Ethiopia has proposed a new way of approaching processes of social mobility.

References

Bennett, Tony, Mike Savage, Elizabeth Silva, Alan Warde, Gayo-Cal. Modesto, and David Wright. 2009. *Culture, Class, Distinction.* New York: Routledge.

Bourdieu, Pierre. 1984. *Distinction: A Social Critique of the Judgment of Taste.* Translated by R. Nice. Cambridge, MA: Harvard University Press.

———. 1986. "The Forms of Capital." In *Handbook of Theory and Research for the Sociology of Education*, edited by John G. Richardson, 241–58. New York: Greenwood Press.

Di Nunzio, Marco. 2019. *The Act of Living: Street Life, Marginality, and Development in Urban Ethiopia.* Cornell University Press.

Friedman, Sam, and Mike Savage. 2017. "Time, Accumulation and Trajectory: Bourdieu and Social Mobility." In *Social Mobility for the 21st Century: Everyone a Winner?* edited by Steph Lawler and Geoff Payne, 1st ed., 67–79. 1 Edition. | New York : Routledge. https://doi.org/10.4324/9781351996808.

Graw, Knut, and Joska Samuli Schielke, eds. 2012. *The Global Horizon: Expectations of Migration in Africa and the Middle East—Google Books.* Leuven University Press.

Heiman, Rachel, Carla Freeman, and Mark Liechty. 2012. "Introduction: Charting an Anthropology of the Middle Classes." In *The Global Middle Classes: Theorizing Through Ethnography*, edited by Rachel Heiman, Carla Freeman, and Mark Liechty, 3–29. Santa Fe: School for Advanced Research Press.

Heinonen, Paula. 2013. *Youth Gangs and Street Children: Culture, Nurture and Masculinity in Ethiopia.* New York: Berghahn Books.

Hull, Elizabeth. 2020. "Going Up or Getting Out? Professional Insecurity and Austerity in the South African Health Sector." *Africa* 90 (3): 548–67. https://doi.org/10.1017/S0001972020000066.

King, Russell. 2012. "Geography and Migration Studies: Retrospect and Prospect." *Population, Space and Place* 18: 134–53.

Lentz, Carola. 2020. "Doing Being Middle-Class in the Global South: Comparative Perspectives and Conceptual Challenges." *Africa* 90 (3): 439–69. https://doi.org/10.1017/S0001972020000029.

Li, Yaojun, Mike Savage, and Alan Warde. 2008. "Social Mobility and Social Capital in Contemporary Britain: Social Mobility and Social Capital in Contemporary Britain." *The British Journal of Sociology* 59 (3): 391–411. https://doi.org/10.1111/j.1468-4446.2008.00200.x.

Liechty, Mark. 2003. *Suitably Modern: Making Middle-Class Culture in a New Consumer Society*. Princeton, NJ: Princeton University Press.
Melber, Henning. 2016. *The Rise of Africa's Middle Class: Myths, Realities and Critical Engagements*. London: Zed Books.
Mercer, Claire, and Charlotte Lemanski. 2020. "The Lived Experiences of the African Middle Classes Introduction." *Africa* 90 (3): 429–38. https://doi.org/10.1017/S0001972020000017.
Nallet, Clélie. 2015. "Classes Moyennes Éthiopiennes Étude Empirique d'une Assignation Catégorielle Incertaine." Doctoral thesis. Bourdeaux: Université de Bourdeaux.
Ortner, Sherry B. 2003. *New Jersey Dreaming: Capital, Culture, and the Class of '58*. Duke University Press.
Prieur, Annick, and Mike Savage. 2013. "Emerging Forms of Cultural Capital." *European Societies* 15 (2): 246–67. https://doi.org/10.1080/14616696.2012.748930.
Savage, Mike, Alan Warde, and Fiona Devine. 2005. "Capitals, Assets, and Resources: Some Critical Issues 1." *The British Journal of Sociology* 56 (1): 31–47.
Skeggs, Beverley. 2015. "Special Issue, Sociologies of Class: Elites (GBCS) and Critiques." *The Sociological Review* 63 (2): 205–549.
Spronk, Rachel. 2012. *Ambiguous Pleasures: Sexuality and Middle Class Self-Perceptions in Nairobi*. New York: Berghahn Books.
———. 2018. "Afterword. The (Idea of) African Middle Classes: Theorizing from Africa." In *Middle Classes in Africa: Changing Lives and Conceptual Challenges*, edited by Lena Kroeker, David O'Kane, and Tabea Scharrer, 311–26. Cham, Switzerland: Palgrave Macmillan.
———. 2020. "Structures, Feelings and *Savoir Faire* : Ghana's Middle Classes in the Making." *Africa* 90 (3): 470–88. https://doi.org/10.1017/S0001972020000030.
Sumich, Jason. 2018. *The Middle Class in Mozambique: The State and the Politics of Transformation in Southern Africa*, vol. 57. Cambridge University Press.
Utsa, Ray. 2014. "Consumption and the Making of the Middle-Class in South Asia." *History Compass* 12 (1): 11–19. https://doi.org/10.1111/hic3.12127.
Vazquez Maggio, Monica Laura. 2017. *Mobility Patterns and Experiences of the Middle Classes in a Globalizing Age: The Case of Mexican Migrants*

in Australia, vol. 6. The Anthropocene: Politik—Economics—Society—Science. Cham: Springer International Publishing. https://doi.org/10.1007/978-3-319-53393-3.

Wacquant, Loic JD. 1991. "Making Class: The Middle Class (Es) in Social Theory and Social Structure." In *Bringing Class Back in: Contemporary and Historical Perspectives*, edited by Scott G. McNall and Rhonda F. Levine, 39–64. Boulder, CO: Westview Press.

Postscript, April 2021

Bleary-eyed at 6 am on Wednesday, 4 November 2020, I was jolted awake by my Twitter feed: a conflict had begun in Tigray. I had spoken to Mehari only a few days before. He had been increasingly concerned about the prospects of war due to provocations from both the Ethiopian government and the regional government of Tigray. The regional government had been unhappy with a series of actions led by the central government: the formation of a new Prosperity Party; the postponement of national elections due to the Covid-19 pandemic; and a rumoured move away from ethnicity-based federal regions with a degree of autonomy towards more centralised rule. These reforms had been increasing the alienation of the TPLF and many Tigrayans, especially as they were accompanied by the arrests of high-profile TPLF officials, the closure of the main road from Addis Ababa to Mekelle (one of the Selam Bus routes) by militias in the Amhara region, and the Prime Minister's stigmatisation of TPLF leaders as 'daytime hyenas.' In protest, local elections were held in Tigray in September 2020 against the will of the Ethiopian government, which in turn prompted further restrictions. Allocated funding to the regional government was frozen, and Tigrayan

M. R. Breines, *Becoming Middle Class*,
Globalization, Urbanization and Development in Africa,
https://doi.org/10.1007/978-981-16-3537-3

athletes were banned from participating in national sporting events. While these and other contentious decisions led to widespread sentiment that a larger conflict was imminent, many—including myself—were taken aback when it actually happened. As I started to make sense of the news that morning, I called several people in Tigray. But I was greeted repeatedly by automated messages saying that the person I was calling was unreachable—a message I would hear many times over the ensuing months.

The Tigray region was plunged into darkness, literally: it was cut off from electricity and all telecommunications. As a consequence, in the first months of the war, very little reliable information reached the outside world about what was going on. Soon, however, rumours flourished on social media about massacres, attacks on civilians, sexual violence, the destruction of churches and mosques, and shortages of food, water and medicine. The Ethiopian government, however, continued to deny most allegations and instead placed the blame for atrocities and any problems occurring in the region on the TPLF. Nevertheless, the fragments of information that have since emerged suggest that heavy fighting rages through much of the Tigray (despite official claims that the operation was concluded after less than a month) and that the situation remains extremely difficult for civilians. For many outside of Tigray who struggle to reach relatives and friends, these have been months of worry and poor sleep as it has been impossible to get word about the safety and well-being of their loved ones.

This book has focused on the role of migration between urban centres in Ethiopia in the formation of a middle class. The research findings have departed from analyses of Ethiopia that tend to be dominated by poverty and conflict, but this new war has made it necessary to revisit some of its findings. On the one hand, migration between urban centres will continue in and between other parts of Ethiopia even as this war continues. On the other, social practices in Tigray have been fundamentally altered as infrastructural conditions and the ongoing fighting limit migration to and from the region. Even if migration out of Tigray is possible in some cases, the sense of betrayal and risks involved in being Tigrayan in other parts of the country has made it a less appealing option. Simultaneously, the violence is disrupting work opportunities, practices of accumulating and sharing wealth with others, and other factors that influence social position. This does not necessarily mean that class relations have simply become irrelevant. Rather, they persist and shape Tigrayans' individual and collective possibilities for getting by, albeit under more tenuous and shifting circumstances.

To keep abreast of my interlocutors' well-being, I have spoken to several of them regularly since the restoration of phone networks in Adigrat. These conversations have informed me about people who have been killed, the looting that has occurred, the interlocutors and acquaintances who have been beaten by soldiers, and the continued fighting taking place in Tigray. One of my interlocutors called me just before midnight in mid-January 2021. I was already asleep but awoke quickly as soon as I heard his voice for the first time in more than two and a half months. Although I had heard from mutual friends who had managed to leave Adigrat and reach Mekelle (where the phone network was restored first) that this person and his family were alive, it was a relief to hear his voice and receive confirmation his family was all indeed relatively well. One of his uncles, who was diabetic, had to have his leg amputated from his thigh downwards due to infection, and another uncle had his house torched, but they were getting by. Another relative fled Humera on the first day of the war and lost all his business assets but managed to return safely to his pregnant wife in Adigrat.

Many of my interlocutors had improved their social and financial position over the years that I had known them, but the violence subjected them to the everyday realities of war, no less than people in other social positions. Soon after conflict erupted, Petros and several of his relatives went to the countryside near the city to hide from the soldiers. He, his wife and young baby spent a month in a small, one-room house together with around 10 other people. There was little food, and water had to be carried from a well some distance away. Everyone slept on the floor, wearing their clothes and shoes, in case soldiers arrived in the night. He explained that eating only once or twice a day was difficult, but that fear made people forget their hunger. Nevertheless, accustomed to a life of relative comfort, with beds, sufficient food, running water and other basic amenities, living under such conditions was very hard for Petros and his family. His wife became very skinny and he himself lost around

10 kilograms. During this time in the countryside, Petros felt that his relative wealth and prosperity did not help him much, as he had no option but to hide outside the city. Nevertheless, he was in a better position than the many others who had to rely on strangers for a place to stay and for food and water, as well as the thousands of people in western Tigray who were forced to flee to Sudan, and the internally displaced who are continuing to arrive empty-handed in cities like Shire, Axum and Adigrat.

Mehari and his family also spent weeks in the mountains during the initial phase of the war. Upon their return to the city after about a month, he found that his business had not been looted, unlike most other offices and non-residential buildings in the city. As soon as the war began, Mehari had taken down the signs for his business to make it appear like a residence and moved valuable goods to another site. Working there came with certain risks because it was in a relatively central location of the city, and Mehari laughed when I asked if he was planning to reopen his business any time soon. He expected that the soldiers would steal all the furniture and equipment and 'leave just the walls behind' if they found out about his assets. Instead of rushing back to work, he thinks of this time as a holiday. This was the first time he has had extended time to rest after having worked hard for several years, and treating it like a break makes it easier to cope with the situation. He has connections who can help him access his savings despite bank closures in Adigrat, which enables him to get by without working for some time. Mehari's relative wealth and continued sharing of his resources with family, relatives and others in need reproduce his position as a person of considerable means even during a time of war.

Petros, on the other hand, found a new routine after he returned to the city. Every morning he walks to his parents' house. There he feeds the family's two remaining oxen and spends time with his elderly parents, siblings and neighbours. He explained that he always rides quickly on his bicycle on the small roads and looks out for soldiers to stay as far away from them as possible because of the risk of unprovoked violence. His wife stays home all day with their baby and her mother, not going outside at all because of the many cases of rape. Petros returns home before 5 pm and then they lock the gate and stay inside until the next day. In the evenings, they have dinner and drink coffee before watching the 9 o'clock news from the Tigray Media House (a diaspora TV channel in the United States). While he assumes that the information about the success of Tigrayan forces on the battlefield is exaggerated in terms of the numbers of Ethiopian and Eritrean soldiers they killed, he finds it to be a source of hope. Despite the fear of violence, life is not too bad for Petros. To some extent, his material possessions, the presence of resourceful relatives and social networks shape how he has been affected by the war. Although his situation is certainly much worse than before the war, his class position has facilitated opportunities that are unavailable to people with less capital.

In early January, Petros travelled to Mekelle and got hold of 15,000 birr (which at the time was worth $375). At that point, he was almost out of cash and had no choice but to go, despite the dangers on the road. In Mekelle, he stocked up on *teff* (grain for making *injera*), rice and pasta for the next three to four months. Upon his return, he shared the money with his parents, siblings and other people who struggled to get by, and pointed out that the money was lasting him a long time because there was hardly anything to spend on because everything was closed. In addition to his savings in the bank, he has a much larger sum of money in *equb* (traditional saving association), but has no idea if he will ever see that money again. Rather than dwelling on possibly having lost most of his money, Petros is happy to be alive and that his family are in good health.

However, he was careful to point out that other people are starving because they have no money and are unable to work because of the destruction and looting. The banks have been closed for months and Petros expects that they will remain closed for a long time. Travelling to Mekelle is very dangerous because of checkpoints and sporadic fighting, making it difficult for those living elsewhere to access their own money. Even though everyone is subject to many of the same limitations in terms of access to food, money, water, health care and other basics, Petros and Mehari's possession and use of capital influence how they manage to get by differently from many others during these difficult times.

Despite the inequalities that exist among Tigrayans, the extreme violence appears to be uniting them in the fight against the Eritrean, Ethiopian and Amhara forces. My interlocutors all expressed a sense of betrayal by Ethiopia. The Ethiopian government's collaboration with Eritrea and the bombing, rape and killing across the region quickly changed many people's sense of national belonging. While the discourses around Tigrayan privilege and related violent incidents had been an issue for Tigrayans in other parts of Ethiopia for many years, the war has made it more common to think that they would be better off if Tigray became an independent nation. One person said that he had not heard of a single person who wanted Tigray to continue being part of a nation that has caused them so much suffering.

These sentiments were also evident in my interlocutors' attitudes towards migration. None of the people in Tigray with whom I have spoken in recent months considered migrating to other parts of Ethiopia. Their shifting sense of citizenship made them prefer to stay in Tigray and seek to rebuild a better future in an independent nation. There were flights to Addis Ababa when Petros was in Mekelle, but he wanted to stay close to his family and friends in Adigrat and did not think it would be any better for him in Addis Ababa or cities in other regions. There was a sense that Ethiopians supported the assaults on Tigrayans, which made it difficult to imagine living in other parts of the country. Unless there is radical change in how the Ethiopian government engages with Tigrayan people and leaders, migration from urban centres in Tigray to the rest of Ethiopia will not resume any time soon.

The only way peace can again prevail in Tigray, my interlocutors argued, is with the expulsion of Ethiopian, Amhara, and Eritrean soldiers from the region, which is why they continued to support the fight against them. This sentiment is also reflected in the steady stream of young people who are joining the Tigrayan forces in the mountains and the continued resistance among the wider population. On the night of 18 February (*Lekatit 11*, an annual celebration of the foundation of the TPLF), there were TPLF flags put up in many places in Adigrat and fireworks all night in defiance of those they saw as invaders, as well as half an hour of gunfire near an army base occupied by Eritrean forces. Such incidents, combined with news of battles across Tigray, give people hope that the war could be won. While they long for victory, they feel sorry for the young Eritrean soldiers, some of whom are as young as 16–18 years old—so small that they struggled to carry their guns—as well as for the young Ethiopian soldiers whom they expect will be quickly killed by the Tigrayan forces. Even as they are fiercely supportive of Tigrayan efforts to drive out the invading soldiers, several of my interlocutors had spent time and made friends in other parts of Ethiopia and had come to know many Eritreans who had sought refuge in Adigrat over the years. As a result, they have mixed feelings and feel sad about the killing of people of other backgrounds who were caught up in this war. Still, Tigrayan ethnicity and solidarity are strengthened through a sense of injustice which overshadows class relations, and differences between ethnic groups become the primary factor in identity production at a time when they feel that they are under attack because of their ethnicity.

After more than five months of the war, fighting still rages in many parts of Tigray and the outcome is far from certain. Massive destruction has taken place across the region and there seems to be no end in sight. Tesfay, who passed away in 2018, was buried on top of a mountain where the monastery of Debre Damo is located, and there have been several reports that this site was shelled by Eritrean artillery. It seems that not even the dead are left in peace. There are countless stories of death, rape and grief, but until now, only trickles have reached the outside world and more harrowing stories are expected in the months and years to come.

The aim of this book has been to provide insights into middle-class lives in Ethiopia. The dramatic events of the past months have cast a shadow over some of its findings as opportunities through urban-to-urban migration have diminished. Nevertheless, interlocutors who had already experienced a degree of social mobility find themselves in better positions than many others—due to their savings and wide social networks—to manage with little or no income for an extended period of time. In other words, class relations continue to influence people's lives at a time that is difficult for everyone. Nonetheless, the changes in Tigray and the region's shifting relationship with the rest of Ethiopia, as well as to Eritrea, will be central in how Tigrayans conceptualise progress and their opportunities for social mobility in the years to come. As the possibilities for urban-to-urban migration are changing, so is middle-class formation. Regardless of these transformations of circumstances, people will continue to find ways to seek better opportunities—both during and after the war.

Index

M. R. Breines, *Becoming Middle Class*,
Globalization, Urbanization and Development in Africa,
https://doi.org/10.1007/978-981-16-3537-3

The manufacturer's authorised representative in the EU is Springer Nature Customer Service Centre GmbH, Europaplatz 3, 69115 Heidelberg, Germany. If you have any concerns regarding our products, please contact ProductSafety@springernature.com

Printed and bound by CPI Group (UK) Ltd, Croydon, CR0 4YY
30/09/2026
02225455-0004